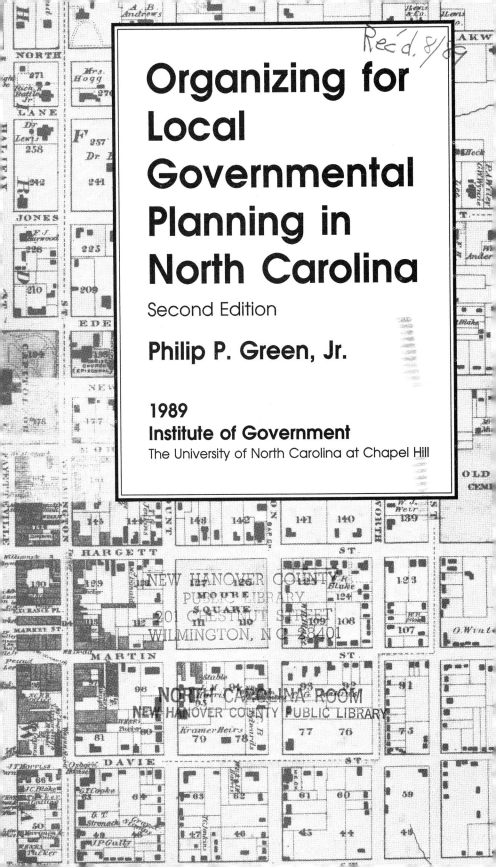

Organizing for Local Governmental Planning in North Carolina

Second Edition

Philip P. Green, Jr.

1989
Institute of Government
The University of North Carolina at Chapel Hill

Contents

Introduction

This book is about organization. More specifically it is about organization within a local government (city or county), designed to carry on a planning function.

It reflects the author's strong beliefs that in organizational matters, form should follow function and that the organizer should make the best use of available resources. In other words, he or she should not organize on the basis of some predetermined pattern—even one that is theoretically best.

Furthermore, a person creating an organization to accomplish given tasks is not engaged in an effort to achieve an artistic organizational chart. Success in organization is reflected in results achieved, not in the symmetry and the clarity of the boxes and the lines of communication on an organization chart.

The focus in this book is upon planning organizations that deal primarily with the *physical development* of a local government's jurisdiction. To be sure, any administrative process may involve planning, but here there is no attention given to planning for delivery of health or social services, planning for law enforcement or fire protection, or planning in connection with any of the internal administrative matters that may concern a manager or a department head.

Finally, the book is cast in macro terms. It does not address the detailed organization of a planning department or a planning staff.

Against this background the discussion of how to organize for local governmental planning must begin with full recognition that there are two major aspects of the problem:

1. Internal organization—what kind of organization is required to meet the needs of a local government for planning within its authorized jurisdiction?

2. Intergovernmental organization—what is an appropriate division of planning functions among the various levels and units of government that share jurisdiction over larger areas with

interlinking concerns? How can their efforts best be coordinated?

Although it is impossible to separate completely the considerations affecting these questions, in general, Part 1 of these materials is concerned with internal organization, and Part 2, with intergovernmental organization.

At the risk of some confusion, Part 1 treats cities and counties together, noting which statutory provisions apply to each. Under the North Carolina statutes there are now almost no differences in the powers and duties of these two general-purpose units of government. Such differences as exist are noted in the text.

Where statutes are involved, these materials describe only the provisions of the General Statutes applying essentially to *all* local units. The reader is cautioned that some local planning organizations or procedures are based upon special acts of the General Assembly applying to only one, or a few, cities or counties. For this reason the reader should check with the local city or county attorney as to the existence of any such legislation before relying upon statements made herein or upon the provisions of the general laws that he or she may find.

Throughout the book the abbreviation *G.S.* refers to the General Statutes of North Carolina. The numbers that follow this designation are chapter and section numbers within the General Statutes, which are commonly combined. Thus, G.S. 160A-360 refers to the 360th section of Chapter 160A of the General Statutes.

Part 1

Internal Organization

1

Historical Evolution of Local Planning

Town Planning

Local governmental planning began, in this country and elsewhere, as "town planning." From very early days, human beings were entranced by the idea of designing not only the structures within which they lived and worked but also the villages, towns, hamlets, and other units within which those structures were clustered.

Most early American town plans were prepared for virginal sites. In North Carolina, town charters during colonial and early post-Revolutionary days typically created a committee of three to five persons and directed it to "lay out" a town on a legally described piece of land. Commonly the charters specified certain ingredients of the town-to-be: streets with certain right-of-way widths; public squares and other open spaces of certain dimensions; sites for a town hall, courthouse, market, and churches; building lots of certain sizes for sale to individuals; and even specifications and materials of the houses that could be built upon the lots. As soon as the plan was prepared—or in some cases, when the lots had been sold—the committee was to fade out of existence.

Later, when private developers such as railroad companies, land speculators, and others began to market land, it was common for them to proceed in the same manner, laying out a plan for their "town" so that potential purchasers could see just how a particular lot might fit into the whole. The approach persists today, in the development of both "new towns" and subdivisions.

The notable feature of this type of town planning is its similarity to the architectural planning of a structure. The planner has information about the shape, the dimensions, and the topography of a piece of land and has a list of the ingredients to be contained in the final plan. Drawing upon his or her knowledge, experience, and imagination, the planner creates a design that best accommodates these factors. There are no people already living there whose wishes have to be taken into account, and the process is one-shot rather than continuing.

Planning in the modern sense of a formal, *continuing* activity of an existing city's government is, in this country, largely a twentieth-century phenomenon. In the latter half of the nineteenth century, a number of notable figures (most with specialties in what is called landscape architecture today) began on a consulting basis to prepare plans for improvement of existing cities—plans for parks, grand boulevards, civic centers, monuments, and the like. In most cases they were hired by local business organizations, civic clubs, or garden clubs. On completion their plans were presented to city leaders with much fanfare and civic enthusiasm. However, local governments had no formal ties to the process of preparing those plans, and officials commonly received the plans and paid no further attention to them.

In 1907 the first formal step was taken to incorporate planning into an American local governmental structure. The city of Hartford, Connecticut, created a Commission on the City Plan composed of appointed citizen members and directed it to oversee the preparation of a plan for the city. This set a pattern. Several "model" enabling acts for planning were drafted in the years that followed (most notably under the aegis of the U.S. Department of Commerce, directed by Secretary Herbert Hoover, in the early 1920s), and they all provided for this type of an appointive board.

Explanatory notes to these model acts painted a picture of a somewhat ivory-tower planning commission, largely independent of the local government it served. It was to be a mechanism through which leading citizens of the community could be given responsibility for the preparation of long-range and broad-gauged plans for the city's development, free of the necessity to enter local political campaigns and free from the distractions of day-to-day problems that engaged the attention of the governing board and administrative officials. Its members were to be appointed for long, staggered terms (so that they would be further insulated from political pressures) and were to have full authority to hire, fire, and direct the activities of their own staff.

It should have been obvious from the beginning perhaps that plans developed in such a hygienic atmosphere would have little influence upon decisions of local officials. However, not until the 1940s did specialists in public administration note this result and begin urging that planning be brought more into the mainstream of local governmental administration. This led to suggestions that units able to afford them should establish full-time planning departments composed of professional planners directly responsible to the manager or the mayor and supported (but not directed) by a citizen planning board. This was to become the prevailing pattern in most cities of 50,000 population or more during the 1950s, 1960s, and 1970s, and in many smaller towns more recently.

At the same time that organization for plan making was taking place, state legislatures began to provide a steady flow of legal tools through which to effectuate plans: zoning, subdivision regulation, mapped-streets protection, minimum-housing-standards ordinances, urban renewal, community development programs, environmental controls, historic preservation ordinances, and so forth. All of these tools in turn required professional and lay personnel for their preparation and use.

In North Carolina there have been examples of all these phases. In the early years of this century, consultants prepared plans for garden clubs, chambers of commerce, and civic clubs in such cities as Asheville, Greensboro, and Raleigh. When it was perceived that a continuing organizational link with local governments was needed, the General Assembly in 1919 authorized cities to create planning boards. The authority was exercised by Greensboro in 1920, Winston-Salem in 1921, Raleigh and Durham in 1922. During the 1920s and 1930s many of the cities with planning boards employed consultants to assist them. The first full-time planning departments in the state emerged in the late 1940s in several of the larger cities—Greensboro, Durham, Winston-Salem, and Raleigh. Beginning in the late 1950s, the state began to provide technical planning assistance to smaller towns that could not afford full-time staffs. In the 1970s some of this responsibility was assumed by regional councils of governments, while the federal Community Development block grant program enabled many towns of 10,000–25,000 population to hire full-time staffs of their own.

County Planning

Throughout the country there has been less interest in, and pressure for, county planning. Rural residents traditionally have been more independent, opposed to governmental direction, and resistant to controls to which urban citizens have long been accustomed. It was not until the coming of the environmental movement, coupled with intrusions of urban development into many previously rural areas (with consequent problems for the farmer and frequently with loss of prime farm lands), that such residents generally perceived a need for planning and land-use regulation.

As county planning programs came into being—initially in such states as Wisconsin in the 1930s—county organization for planning tended to mimic that of cities. Most counties began their efforts with appointed planning boards or commissions, supported by part-time consultant staffs. Gradually the larger and more urban counties replaced these with full-time departments.

In North Carolina, counties were first authorized to create planning boards in 1945, but no use was made of this authority until the 1959 General Assembly added power for counties to zone and regulate subdivisions (a few large counties such as Forsyth, Durham, and Mecklenburg operated earlier under special acts of the General Assembly). This authority, plus later inducements in the form of Farmers Home Administration water-and-sewerage-system grants and Community Development block grants that were made contingent upon the existence of a local planning program, led to a steady growth in the number of counties with planning programs. Most counties have relied upon assistance from the state's Department of Natural Resources and Community Development and from regional organizations for professional planning staff support. However, in the 1970s a growing number of counties with midrange populations joined the larger counties in creating full-time planning departments.

Traditional Elements of Local Planning Organizations

As the preceding discussion indicates, traditional elements of local planning organizations have been as follows:

1. A *governing board* to create the entire organization and provide it with personnel, equipment, finances, and other support. This board has had additional responsibilities for carrying out plans by adopting and amending land-use regulations, administering certain of those regulations, and mandating (and appropriating funds for) public projects called for by those plans.

2. A *planning board and support staff* with primary responsibility for preparing and adopting plans (including all necessary studies), developing and recommending ordinances to effectuate those plans, recommending amendments to those

ordinances, helping to administer subdivision regulations and perhaps the zoning ordinance, and developing policies for adoption by the governing board and for use in its decision making.

3. Various *officials, agencies, and departments* engaged in activities required to carry out plans. In addition to those mentioned earlier, these might include an interdepartmental coordinating committee, a city or county engineer, a health department, an inspection department, a zoning board of adjustment, a department of public works, a housing authority, a redevelopment commission, a department of community development, a historic district commission, a historic properties commission, an appearance commission, an economic development commission, etc.

As in most states, in North Carolina the General Assembly has traditionally *authorized* local planning agencies rather than *mandating* them. However, in the early years, if a local government chose to exercise certain powers, it was *required* to have specified organizational units—and the statutes mandated some matters with needless exactitude. For example, before 1971 a North Carolina town had to create a planning board if it wished (a) to adopt and amend a zoning ordinance, (b) to adopt and administer subdivision regulations, (c) to carry on an urban renewal program, or (d) to prepare and carry out an economic development program. Further, this planning board had to have from three to nine members, and it had to make an annual report to the governing board. If a town zoned extraterritorially, it had to double the size of its planning board and board of adjustment by adding residents of extraterritorial areas. A county had to have a planning board with as many members as it had townships (but not less than three) if it wished to engage in any of these activities. All of the mandatory requirements just described were loosened in 1971 and 1973, when the General Assembly rewrote the basic city and county laws of the state.

2

Current State Statutes Affecting Organization for Local Planning

When most of North Carolina's general laws relating to municipalities were rewritten as Chapter 160A of the General Statutes in 1971 and the laws relating to counties were rewritten as Chapter 153A in 1973, the General Assembly took quite a different approach to planning legislation. Instead of *mandating* particular features, these statutes were written as true *enabling* legislation. To the greatest degree possible, the statutes *authorized* local governments to engage in specified activities while giving them maximum freedom to organize for those activities in the manner that the city council or the board of county commissioners deemed most suitable.

The following statutory provisions indicate this new freedom. *Because of their length, the casual reader will probably wish to look over them quickly, returning to study only those of particular importance to him or her.*

Statutory Provisions

Municipal

G.S. 160A-146.   Council to organize city government.

The council may create, change, abolish, and consolidate offices, positions, departments, boards, commissions, and agencies of the city government and generally organize and reorganize the city government in order to promote orderly and efficient administration of city affairs, subject to the following limitations:

(1) The council may not abolish any office, position, department, board, commission, or agency established and required by law;

(2) The council may not combine offices or confer certain duties on the same officer when such action is specifically forbidden by law;

(3) The council may not discontinue or assign elsewhere any functions or duties assigned by law to a particular office, position, department, or agency.

G.S. 160A-361.   Planning agency.

Any city may by ordinance create or designate one or more agencies to perform the following duties:

(1) Make studies of the area within its jurisdiction and surrounding areas;

(2) Determine objectives to be sought in the development of the study area;

(3) Prepare and adopt plans for achieving these objectives;

(4) Develop and recommend policies, ordinances, administrative procedures, and other means for carrying out plans in a coordinated and efficient manner;

(5) Advise the council concerning the use and amendment of means for carrying out plans;

(6) Exercise any functions in the administration and enforcement of various means for carrying out plans that the council may direct;

(7) Perform any other related duties that the council may direct.

An agency created or designated pursuant to this section may include, but shall not be limited to, one or more of the following, with such staff as the council may deem appropriate:

(1) A planning board or commission of any size (not less than three members) or composition deemed appropriate, organized in any manner deemed appropriate;

(2) A joint planning board created by two or more local governments pursuant to Article 20, Part 1, of this Chapter.

G.S. 160A-362.   Extraterritorial representation.

When a city elects to exercise extraterritorial zoning or subdivision-regulation powers under G.S. 160A-360, it shall in the ordinance creating or designating its planning agency or agencies provide a means of representation for residents of the extraterritorial area to be regulated. Representation shall be provided by appointing residents of the area to the planning agency and the board of adjustment that makes recommendations or grants relief in these matters. Any advisory board established prior to July 1, 1983, to provide the required extraterritorial representation shall constitute compliance with this section until the board is abolished by ordinance of the city. The representatives on the planning agency and the board of adjustment shall be appointed by the board of county commissioners with jurisdiction over the area. If there is an insufficient number of qualified residents of the area to meet membership requirements, the board of county commissioners may appoint as many other residents of the county as necessary to make up the requisite number. When the extraterritorial area extends into two or more counties, each board of county commissioners concerned shall appoint representatives from its portion of the area, as specified in the ordinance. If a board of county commissioners fails to make these appointments within 90 days after receiving a resolution from the city council requesting that they be made, the city council may make them. If the ordinance so provides, the outside representatives may have equal rights, privileges, and duties with the other members of the agency to which they are appointed, regardless of whether the matters at issue arise within the city or within the extraterritorial area; otherwise they shall function only with respect to matters within the extraterritorial area.

G.S. 160A-363.   Supplemental powers.

A city or its designated planning agency may accept, receive, and disburse in furtherance of its functions any funds, grants, and services made available by the federal government and its agencies, the State government and its agencies, any local government and its agencies, and any private and civic sources. Any city, or its designated planning agency with the concurrence of the council, may enter into and carry out contracts with the State and federal governments or any agencies thereof under which financial or other planning assistance is made available to the city and may agree to and comply with any reasonable conditions that are imposed upon such assistance.

Any city, or its designated planning agency with the concurrence of the council, may enter into and carry out contracts with any other city, county, or regional council or planning agency under which it agrees to furnish technical planning assistance to the other local government or planning agency. Any city, or its designated planning agency with the concurrence of its council, may enter into and carry out contracts with any other city, county, or regional council or planning agency under which it agrees to pay the other local government or planning agency for technical planning assistance.

Any city council is authorized to make any appropriations that may be necessary to carry out any activities or contracts authorized by this Article or to support, and compensate members of, any planning agency that it may create pursuant to this Article, and to levy taxes for these purposes as a necessary expense.

County

G.S. 153A-76.   Board of commissioners to organize county government.

The board of commissioners may create, change, abolish, and consolidate offices, positions, departments, boards, commissions, and agencies of the county government, may impose ex officio the duties of more than one office on a single officer, may change the composition and manner of selection of boards, commissions, and agencies, and may generally organize and reorganize the county government in order to promote orderly and efficient administration of county affairs, subject to the following limitations:

(1) The board may not abolish an office, position, department, board, commission, or agency established or required by law.

(2) The board may not combine offices or confer certain duties on the same officer when this action is specifically forbidden by law.

(3) The board may not discontinue or assign elsewhere a function or duty assigned by law to a particular office, position, department, board, commission, or agency.

(4) The board may not change the composition or manner of selection of a local board of education, the board of health, the board of social services, the board of elections, or the board of alcoholic beverage control.

G.S. 153A-321. Planning agency.

A county may by ordinance create or designate one or more agencies to perform the following duties:

(1) Make studies of the county and surrounding areas;

(2) Determine objectives to be sought in the development of the study area;

(3) Prepare and adopt plans for achieving these objectives;

(4) Develop and recommend policies, ordinances, administrative procedures, and other means for carrying out plans in a coordinated and efficient manner;

(5) Advise the board of commissioners concerning the use and amendment of means for carrying out plans;

(6) Exercise any functions in the administration and enforcement of various means for carrying out plans that the board of commissioners may direct;

(7) Perform any other related duties that the board of commissioners may direct.

An agency created or designated pursuant to this section may include but shall not be limited to one or more of the following, with any staff that the board of commissioners considers appropriate:

(1) A planning board or commission of any size (not less than three members) or composition considered appropriate, organized in any manner considered appropriate;

(2) A joint planning board created by two or more local governments according to the procedures and provisions of Chapter 160A, Article 20, Part 1.

G.S. 153A-322. Supplemental powers.

A county or its designated planning agency may accept, receive, and disburse in furtherance of its functions funds, grants, and services made available by the federal government or its agencies, the State government or its agencies, any local government or its agencies, and private or civic sources. A county, or its designated planning agency with the concurrence of the board of commissioners, may enter into and carry out contracts with the State or federal governments or any agencies of either under which financial or other planning assistance is made available to the county and may agree to and comply with any reasonable conditions that are imposed upon the assistance.

A county, or its designated planning agency with the concurrence of the board of commissioners, may enter into and carry out contracts with any other county, city, regional council, or planning agency under which it agrees to furnish technical planning assistance to the other local government or planning agency. A county, or its designated planning agency with the concurrence of the board of commissioners, may enter into and carry out contracts with any other county, city, regional council, or planning agency under which it agrees to pay the other local government or planning agency for technical planning assistance.

A county may make any appropriations that may be necessary to carry out an activity or contract authorized by this Article, by Chapter 157A, or by Chapter 160A, Article 19 or to support, and compensate members of, any planning agency that it may create or designate pursuant to this Article.

The reader should note that G.S. 160A-361 and G.S. 153A-321 authorize "one *or more*" (italics added) planning agencies and that they specifically authorize (but do not require) "a planning board or commission" as *one* such agency (without imposing a maximum size, dictating from whence appointees must come, or specifying internal organization and staff support). The reader should also note that of the list of duties that may be assigned to one or more planning agencies pursuant to G.S. 160A-361 and G.S. 153A-321, items (*1*), (*2*), (*3*), and (*4*) are plan-making functions of the types traditionally assigned to a planning board and staff, whereas (*5*) and (*6*) are plan-effectuation functions of the types traditionally assigned to a variety of boards, departments, and officials (among whom might be listed the planning board and its staff, the governing board, the zoning board of adjustment, the zoning administrator, the inspection department, and many other agencies). Therefore, if a particular government wishes to continue with the same organization that it has had over the years, it may do so, but it is also free to modify that organization if it feels that improvement would result.

Related Statutory Provisions

Not all of North Carolina's statutes use the new terminology. The rewritten enabling acts for city and county zoning, historic districts, historic properties commissions, and subdivision regulation (G.S. Chapter 160A, Article 19, Parts 2, 3, 3A, and 3B; G.S. Chapter 153A, Article 18, Parts 2 and 3) all mention a "planning agency," but they mention other organizational entities as well. Other acts do not refer to a "planning agency" at all; they mandate other entities.

Some of the provisions pertaining to the major organizational entities mentioned in the statutes are shown below. (Excerpts from the statutes are only long enough to give the reader a general understanding of the composition, the powers, and the duties of the authorized agency.) Taken in conjunction with the broad authority granted to cities and counties by the statutes set forth at the beginning of the chapter, this range of more specialized provisions reinforces the view that the General Assembly wishes to give maximum flexibility to local governments to organize in the manner best suited to their circumstances.

Zoning

Municipal

G.S. 160A-381.   Grant of power.

For the purpose of promoting health, safety, morals, or the general welfare of the community, any city may regulate and restrict the height, number of stories and size of buildings and other structures, the percentage of lots that may be occupied, the size of yards, courts and other open spaces, the density of population, and the location and use of buildings, structures and land for trade, industry, residence or other purposes. . . . These regulations may provide that a board of adjustment may determine and vary their application in harmony with their general purpose and intent and in accordance with general or specific rules therein contained. The regulations may also provide that the board of adjustment or the city council may issue special use permits or conditional use permits in the classes of cases or situations and in accordance with the principles, conditions, safeguards, and procedures specified therein and may impose reasonable and appropriate conditions and safeguards upon these permits. . . .

G.S. 160A-387.   Planning agency; zoning plan; certification to city council.

In order to exercise the powers conferred by this Part, a city council shall create or designate a planning agency under the provisions of this Article or of a special act of the General Assembly. The planning agency shall prepare a proposed zoning ordinance, including both the full text of such ordinance and maps showing proposed district boundaries. The planning agency may hold public hearings in the course of preparing the ordinance. Upon completion, the planning agency shall certify the ordinance to the city council. The city council shall not hold its required public hearing or take action until it has received a certified ordinance from the planning agency. Following its required public hearing, the city council may refer the ordinance back to the planning agency for any further recommendations that the agency may wish to make prior to final action by the city council in adopting, modifying and adopting, or rejecting the ordinance.

G.S. 160A-388.   Board of adjustment.

(a) The city council may provide for the appointment and compensation of a board of adjustment consisting of five or more members, each to be appointed for three years. In appointing the original members of such board, or in the filling of vacancies caused by the expiration of the terms of existing members, the council may appoint certain members for less than three years to the end that thereafter the terms of all members shall not expire at the same time. The council may, in its discretion, appoint and provide compensation for alternate members to serve on the board in the absence of any regular member. . . . A city may designate a planning agency to perform any or all of the duties of a board of adjustment in addition to its other duties.

(b) The board of adjustment shall hear and decide appeals from and review any order, requirement, decision, or determination made by an administrative official charged with the enforcement of any ordinance adopted pursuant to this Part. . . . The board of adjustment shall fix a reasonable time for the hearing of the appeal, give due notice thereof to the parties, and decide it within a reasonable time. The board of adjustment may reverse or affirm, wholly or partly, or may modify the order, requirement, decision, or determination appealed from, and shall make any order, requirement, decision, or determination that in its opinion ought to be made in the premises. To this end the board shall have all the powers of the officer from whom the appeal is taken.

(c) The zoning ordinance may provide that the board of adjustment may permit special exceptions to the zoning regulations in classes of cases or situations and in accordance with the principles, conditions, safeguards, and procedures specified in the ordinance. The ordinance may also authorize the board to interpret zoning maps and pass upon disputed questions of lot lines or district boundary lines and similar questions as they arise in the administration of the ordinance. The board shall hear and decide all matters referred to it or upon which it is required to pass under any zoning ordinance.

(d) When practical difficulties or unnecessary hardships would result from carrying out the strict letter of a zoning ordinance, the board of adjustment shall have the power, in passing upon appeals, to vary or modify any of the regulations or provisions of the ordinance relating to the use, construction or alteration of buildings or structures or the use of land, so that the spirit of the ordinance shall be observed, public safety and welfare secured, and substantial justice done.

(e) The concurring vote of four-fifths of the members of the board shall be necessary to reverse any order, requirement, decision, or determination of any administrative official charged with the enforcement of an ordinance adopted pursuant to this Part, or to decide in favor of the applicant any matter upon which it is required to pass under any ordinance, or to grant a variance from the provisions of the ordinance. Every decision of the board shall be subject to review by the superior court by proceedings in the nature of certiorari. . . .

County

G.S. 153A-340.   Grant of power.

For the purpose of promoting health, safety, morals, or the general welfare, a county may regulate and restrict the height, number of stories and size of buildings and other structures, the percentage of lots that may be occupied, the size of yards, courts and other open spaces, the density of population, and the location and use of buildings, structures, and land for trade, industry, residence, or other purposes. . . .

. . . The regulations may provide that a board of adjustment may determine and vary their application in harmony with their general purpose and intent and in accordance with general or specific rules therein contained. The regulations may also provide that the board of adjustment or the board of commissioners may issue special use permits or conditional use permits in the classes of cases or situations and in accordance with the principles, conditions, safeguards, and procedures specified therein and may impose reasonable and appropriate conditions and safeguards upon these permits. . . .

G.S. 153A-344.   Planning agency; zoning plan; certification to board of commissioners; amendments.

(a) To exercise the powers conferred by this Part, a county shall create or designate a planning agency under the provisions of this

Article or of a local act. The planning agency shall prepare a proposed zoning ordinance, including both the full text of such ordinance and maps showing proposed district boundaries. The planning agency may hold public hearings in the course of preparing the ordinance. Upon completion, the planning agency shall certify the ordinance to the board of commissioners. The board of commissioners shall not hold the public hearing required by G.S. 153A-323 or take action until it has received a certified ordinance from the planning agency. Following its required public hearing, the board of commissioners may refer the ordinance back to the planning agency for any further recommendations that the agency may wish to make prior to final action by the board in adopting, modifying and adopting, or rejecting the ordinance.

Zoning regulations and restrictions and zone boundaries may from time to time be amended, supplemented, changed, modified, or repealed. . . . Before an amendment may be adopted, it must be referred to the planning agency for the agency's recommendation. The agency shall be given at least 30 days in which to make a recommendation. The board of commissioners is not bound by the recommendations, if any, of the planning agency. . . .

G.S. 153A-345.   Board of adjustment.

(a) The board of commissioners may provide for the appointment and compensation, if any, of a board of adjustment consisting of at least five members, each to be appointed for three years. . . . The board of commissioners may provide for the appointment and compensation, if any, of alternate members to serve on the board in the absence of any regular member. . . . If the board of commissioners does not zone the entire territorial jurisdiction of the county, each designated zoning area shall have at least one resident as a member of the board of adjustment.

A county may designate a planning agency to perform any or all of the duties of a board of adjustment in addition to its other duties.

(b) The board of adjustment shall hear and decide appeals from and review any order, requirement, decision, or determination made by an administrative official charged with enforcing an ordinance adopted pursuant to this Part. . . . The board of adjustment shall fix a reasonable time for the hearing of the appeal, give due notice of the appeal to the parties, and decide the appeal within a reasonable time. The board of adjustment may reverse or affirm, in whole or in part, or may modify the order, requirement, decision, or determination appealed from, and shall make any order, requirement, decision, or determination that in its opinion ought to be made in the circumstances. To this end the board has all of the powers of the officer from whom the appeal is taken.

(c) The zoning ordinance may provide that the board of adjustment may permit special exceptions to the zoning regulations in classes of cases or situations and in accordance with the principles, conditions, safeguards, and procedures specified in the ordinance. The ordinance may also authorize the board to interpret zoning maps and pass upon disputed questions of lot lines or district boundary lines and similar questions that may arise in the administration of the ordinance. The board shall hear and decide all matters referred to it or upon which it is required to pass under the zoning ordinance.

(d) When practical difficulties or unnecessary hardships would result from carrying out the strict letter of a zoning ordinance, the board of adjustment may, in passing upon appeals, vary or modify any regulation or provision of the ordinance relating to the use, construction, or alteration of buildings or structures or the use of land, so that the spirit of the ordinance is observed, public safety and welfare secured, and substantial justice done.

(e) The board of adjustment, by a vote of four-fifths of its members, may reverse any order, requirement, decision, or determination of an administrative officer charged with enforcing an ordinance adopted pursuant to this Part, or may decide in favor of the applicant a matter upon which the board is required to pass under the ordinance, or may grant a variance from the provisions of the ordinance. Each decision of the board is subject to review by the superior court by proceedings in the nature of certiorari. . . .

Airport Zoning

Municipal, County, or Airport Authority

G.S. 63-31.   Adoption of airport zoning regulations.

(a) Every political subdivision may adopt, administer, and enforce . . . airport zoning regulations, which regulations shall divide the area surrounding any airport within the jurisdiction of said political subdivision into zones, and, within such zones, specify the land uses permitted, and regulate and restrict the height to which structures and trees may be erected or allowed to grow. . . .

(b) In the event that a political subdivision has adopted . . . a general zoning ordinance regulating, among other things, the height of buildings, any airport zoning regulations adopted for the same area or portion thereof under this Article may be incorporated in and made a part of such general zoning regulations . . . .

(c) Any two or more political subdivisions may agree, by ordinance duly adopted, to create a joint board and delegate to said board the powers herein conferred to promulgate, administer and enforce airport zoning regulations to protect the aerial approaches of any airport located within the corporate limits of any one or more of said political subdivisions. Such joint board shall have as members two representatives appointed by the chief executive officer of each political subdivision participating in the creation of said board and a chairman elected by a majority of the members so appointed.

(d) The jurisdiction of each political subdivision is hereby extended to the promulgating, adopting, administering and enforcement of airport zoning regulations to protect the approaches of any airport or landing field which is owned by said political subdivision, although the area affected by the zoning regulations may be located outside the corporate limits of said political subdivision. In case of conflict with any airport zoning or other regulations promulgated by any political subdivision, the regulations adopted pursuant to this section shall prevail. . . .

G.S. 63-33.　　Procedure.

(a) Adoption of Zoning Regulations.—No airport zoning regulations shall be adopted, amended, or changed under this Article except by action of the legislative body of the political subdivision in question, or the joint board provided for in G.S. 63-31, subsection (c), after a public hearing in relation thereto . . . .

(b) Administration of Zoning Regulations—Administrative Agency.— The legislative body of any political subdivision adopting airport zoning regulations under this Article may delegate the duty of administering and enforcing such regulations to any administrative agency under its jurisdiction, or may create a new administrative agency to perform such duty, but such administrative agency shall not be or include any member of the board of appeals. The duties of such administrative agency shall include that of hearing and deciding all permits . . . but such agency shall not have or exercise any of the powers delegated to the board of appeals.

(c) Administration of Airport Zoning Regulations—Board of Appeals.—Airport zoning regulations adopted under this Article shall provide for a board of appeals to have and exercise the following powers:

(1) To hear and decide appeals from any order, requirement, decision, or determination made by the administrative agency in the enforcement of this Article or of any ordinance adopted pursuant thereto;

(2) To hear and decide special exceptions to the terms of the ordinance upon which such board may be required to pass under such ordinance;

(3) To hear and decide specific variances . . . .

Where a zoning board of appeals or adjustment already exists, it may be appointed as the board of appeals. Otherwise, the board of appeals shall consist of five members, each to be appointed for a term of three years and to be removable for cause by the appointing authority upon written charges and after public hearing. . . .

Subdivision Regulation

Municipal

G.S. 160A-371.   Subdivision regulation.

A city may by ordinance regulate the subdivision of land within its territorial jurisdiction.

G.S. 160A-373.   Ordinance to contain procedure for plat approval; approval prerequisite to plat recordation; statement by owner.

Any subdivision ordinance adopted pursuant to this Part shall contain provisions setting forth the procedures to be followed in granting or denying approval of a subdivision plat prior to its registration.

The ordinance may provide that final approval of each individual subdivision plat is to be given by

(1) The city council,

(2) The city council on recommendation of a planning agency, or

(3) A designated planning agency.

From and after the time that a subdivision ordinance is filed with the register of deeds of the county, no subdivision plat of land within the city's jurisdiction shall be filed or recorded until it shall have been submitted to and approved by the appropriate agency, as specified in the subdivision ordinance, and until this approval shall have been entered on the face of the plat in writing by the chairman or head of the agency. The register of deeds shall not file or record a plat of a subdivision of land located within the territorial jurisdiction of a city that has not been approved in accordance with these provisions, nor shall the clerk of superior court order or direct the recording of a plat if the recording would be in conflict with this section. The owner of land shown on a subdivision plat submitted for recording, or his authorized agent, shall sign a statement on the plat stating whether or not any land shown thereon is within the subdivision-regulation jurisdiction of any city.

County

G.S. 153A-330.   Subdivision regulation.

A county may by ordinance regulate the subdivision of land within its territorial jurisdiction. If a county, pursuant to G.S. 153A-342, has adopted a zoning ordinance that applies only to one or more designated portions of its territorial jurisdiction, it may adopt subdivision regulations that apply only within the areas so zoned and need not regulate the subdivision of land in the rest of its jurisdiction.

G.S. 153A-332.   **Ordinance to contain procedure for plat approval; approval prerequisite to plat recordation; statement by owner.**

A subdivision ordinance adopted pursuant to this Part shall contain provisions setting forth the procedures to be followed in granting or denying approval of a subdivision plat before its registration.

The ordinance shall provide that the following agencies be given an opportunity to make recommendations concerning an individual sub-division plat before the plat is approved:

(1) The district highway engineer as to proposed streets, highways, and drainage systems;

(2) The county health director as to proposed water or sewerage systems;

(3) Any other agency or official designated by the board of commis-sioners.

The ordinance may provide that final approval of each individual subdivision plat is to be given by:

(1) The board of commissioners,

(2) The board of commissioners on recommendation of a planning agency, or

(3) A designated planning agency.

From the time that a subdivision ordinance is filed with the register of deeds of the county, no subdivision plat of land within the county's jurisdiction may be filed or recorded until it has been submitted to and approved by the appropriate board or agency, as specified in the subdi-vision ordinance, and until this approval is entered in writing on the face of the plat by the chairman or head of the board or agency. The register of deeds may not file or record a plat of a subdivision of land located within the territorial jurisdiction of the county that has not been approved in accordance with these provisions, and the clerk of superior court may not order or direct the recording of a plat if the recording would be in conflict with this section. The owner of land shown on a subdivision plat submitted for recording, or his authorized agent, shall sign a statement on the plat stating whether any land shown thereon is within the subdivision-regulation jurisdiction of the county.

Historic Districts

Municipal, County, or Joint

G.S. 160A-395.   **Exercise of powers under this Part by counties as well as cities; designation of historic districts.**

The term "municipality" or "municipal" as used in G.S. 160A-395 through 160A-399 shall be deemed to include the governing board or legislative board of a county, to the end that counties may exercise the same powers as cities with respect to the establishment of historic districts.

Any such legislative body may, as part of a zoning ordinance enacted or amended pursuant to this Article, designate and from time to time amend one or more historic districts within the area subject to the ordinance. Such ordinance may treat historic districts either as a separate use-district classification or as districts which overlay other zoning districts. Where historic districts are designated as separate-use districts, the zoning ordinance may include as uses by right or as conditional uses those uses found by the historic district commission to have existed during the period sought to be restored or preserved, or to be compatible with the restoration or preservation of the district. No historic district or districts shall be designated until:

(1) An investigation and report describing the significance of the buildings, structures, features, sites or surroundings included in any such proposed district, and a description of the boundaries of such district has been prepared; and

(2) The Department of Cultural Resources, acting through an agent or employee designated by its Secretary, shall have made an analysis of and recommendations concerning such report and description of proposed boundaries. Failure of the Department to submit its written analysis and recommendations to the municipal governing body within 30 calendar days after a written request for such analysis has been mailed to it shall relieve the municipality of any responsibility for awaiting such analysis, and said body may at any time thereafter take any necessary action to adopt or amend its zoning ordinance.

The municipal governing body may also, in its discretion, refer the report and proposed boundaries to any local historic properties commission or other interested body for its recommendations prior to taking action to amend the zoning ordinance. . . .

On receipt of these reports and recommendations, the municipality may proceed in the same manner as would otherwise be required for the adoption or amendment of any appropriate zoning ordinance provisions.

G.S. 160A-396.   Historic district commission.

Before it may designate one or more historic districts, a municipality shall establish or designate a historic district commission. The municipal governing board shall determine the number of members of the commission, which shall be at least three, and the length of their terms, which shall be no greater than four years. A majority of the members of such a commission shall have demonstrated special interest, experience, or education in history or architecture; and all the members shall reside within the territorial jurisdiction of the municipality as established pursuant to G.S. 160A-360.

In lieu of establishing a separate historic district commission, a municipality may designate as its historic district commission, (i) a historic properties commission established pursuant to G.S. 160A-399.2, (ii) a planning agency established pursuant to G.S. 160A-361, or (iii) a community appearance commission established pursuant to Part 7 of this Article. In order for a commission or board other than the historic district commission to be designated, at least two of its members shall have demonstrated special interest, experience, or education in history or architecture. At the discretion of the municipality the ordinance may also provide that the historic district commission may exercise within a historic district any or all of the powers of a planning agency or a community appearance commission.

A county and one or more cities in the county may establish or designate a joint historic district commission. If a joint commission is established or designated, the county and cities involved shall determine the residence requirements of members of the joint historic district commission.

G.S. 160A-397. Certificate of appropriateness required.

From and after the designation of a historic district, no exterior portion of any building or other structure (including masonry walls, fences, light fixtures, steps and pavement, or other appurtenant features) nor above-ground utility structure nor any type of outdoor advertising sign shall be erected, altered, restored, moved or demolished within such district until after an application for a certificate of appropriateness as to exterior features has been submitted to and approved by the historic district commission. The municipality shall require such a certificate to be issued by the commission prior to the issuance of a building permit or other permit granted for the purposes of constructing, altering, moving or demolishing structures, which certificate may be issued subject to reasonable conditions necessary to carry out the purposes of this Part. A certificate of appropriateness shall be required whether or not a building or other permit is required. . . .

. . . An appeal may be taken to the Board of Adjustment from the commission's action in granting or denying any certificate . . . . Any appeal from the Board of Adjustment's decision in any such case shall be heard by the superior court of the county in which the municipality is located. . . .

G.S. 160A-399. Delay in demolition of buildings within historic district.

An application for a certificate of appropriateness authorizing the demolition of a building or structure within the district may not be denied. However, the effective date of such a certificate may be delayed for a period of up to 180 days from the date of approval. . . . During such period the historic district commission may negotiate with the owner and with any other parties in an effort to find a means of preserving the building. If the historic district commission finds that the building has no particular significance or value toward maintaining the character of the district, it shall waive all or part of such period and authorize earlier demolition or removal.

Historic Properties Commission

Municipal, County, or Joint

G.S. 160A-399.2. Appointment or designation of historic properties commission.

Before it may exercise the powers set forth in this Part, a municipality shall establish or designate a historic properties commission. The municipality's governing board shall determine the number of members of the commission, which shall be at least three, and the length of their terms, which shall be no greater than four years. A majority of the members of such a commission shall have demonstrated special interest, experience, or education in history or architecture; and all the members shall reside within the territorial jurisdiction of the city or county as established pursuant to G.S. 160A-360. In establishing such a commission and making appointments to it, a city or county may seek the advice of any State or local historical or preservation agency, or organization.

In lieu of establishing a separate historic properties commission, a municipality may designate as its historic properties commission either (i) the city or county historic district commission, established pursuant to G.S. 160A-396, or (ii) a city or county planning agency. In order for a planning agency to be designated, at least two of its members shall have demonstrated special interest, experience, or education in history or architecture.

A county and one or more cities in the county may establish or designate a joint historic properties commission. If a joint commission is established, the county and city or cities involved shall determine the residence requirements for members of the joint historic properties commission.

G.S. 160A-399.3. Powers of the properties commission.

Any historic properties commission established pursuant to this Part shall be authorized within the zoning jurisdiction of the unit to:

(1) Undertake an inventory of properties of historical, architectural and/or archaeological significance;

(2) Recommend to the municipal governing board structures, buildings, sites, areas or objects to be designated by ordinance as "historic properties";

(3) Acquire by any lawful means the fee or any lesser included interest, including options to purchase, to any such historic properties, to hold, manage, preserve, restore and improve the same, and to exchange or dispose of the property by public or private sale, lease or otherwise, subject to covenants or other legally binding restrictions which will secure appropriate rights of public access and promote the preservation of the property;

(4) Restore, preserve and operate such historic properties;

(5) Recommend to the governing board that designation of any building, structure, site, area or object as a historic property be revoked or removed;

(6) Conduct an educational program with respect to historic properties within its jurisdiction;

(7) Cooperate with the State, federal and local governments in pursuance of the purposes of this Part. The governing board or the commission when authorized by the governing board may contract with the State, or the United States of America, or any agency of either, or with any other organization provided the terms are not inconsistent with State or federal law;

(8) Enter, solely in performance of its official duties and only at reasonable times, upon private lands for examination or survey thereof. However, no member, employee or agent of the commission may enter any private building or structure without the express consent of the owner or occupant thereof.

G.S. 160A-399.5. Required procedures.

As a guide for the identification and evaluation of historic properties, the commission shall undertake, at the earliest possible time and consistent with the resources available to it, an inventory of properties of historical, architectural and cultural significance within its jurisdiction. Such inventories and any additions or revisions thereof shall be submitted as expeditiously as possible to the Division of Archives and History. No ordinance designating a historic building, structure, site, area or object nor any amendment thereto may be adopted, nor may any property be accepted or acquired by a historic properties commission or the governing board of a municipality, until the following procedural steps have been taken:

(1) The historic properties commission shall (i) prepare and adopt rules of procedure, and (ii) prepare and adopt principles and guidelines, not inconsistent with this Part, for altering, restoring, moving or demolishing properties designated as historic.

(2) The historic properties commission shall make or cause to be made an investigation and report on the historic, architectural,

educational or cultural significance of each building, structure, site, area or object proposed for designation or acquisition. Such investigation or report shall be forwarded to the Division of Archives and History, North Carolina Department of Cultural Resources.

(3) The Department of Cultural Resources, acting through any employee designated by the secretary of the North Carolina Historical Commission shall either upon request of the Department or at the initiative of the historic properties commission be given an opportunity to review and comment upon the substance and effect of the designation of any historic property pursuant to this Part. . . . If the Department does not submit its comments or recommendations in connection with any designation within 30 days following receipt by the Department of the investigation and report of the commission, the commission and any city or county governing board shall be relieved of any responsibility to consider such comments.

(4) The historic properties commission and the governing board shall hold a joint public hearing or separate public hearings on the proposed ordinance. . . .

(5) Following the joint public hearing or separate public hearings, the governing board may adopt the ordinance as proposed, adopt the ordinance with any amendments it deems necessary, or reject the proposed ordinance.

(6) Upon adoption of the ordinance, the owners and occupants of each designated historic property shall be given written notification of such designation insofar as reasonable diligence permits. One copy of the ordinance and all amendments thereto shall be filed by the historic properties commission in the office of the register of deeds of the county in which the property or properties are located. . . . In the case of any property lying within the zoning jurisdiction of a city, a second copy of the ordinance and all amendments thereto shall be kept on file in the office of the city or town clerk and be made available for public inspection at any reasonable time. A third copy of the ordinance and all amendments thereto shall be given to the city or county building inspector. . . .

(7) Upon the adoption of the historic properties ordinance or any amendment thereto, it shall be the duty of the historic properties commission to give notice thereof to the tax supervisor of the county in which the property is located. . . .

G.S. 160A-399.6. Certificate of appropriateness required.

A property which has been designated as a historic property as herein provided may be materially altered, restored, moved or demolished only following the issuance of a certificate of appropriateness by the historic properties commission in accordance with the procedures and standards set forth in Part 3A of this Article. . . .

G.S. 160A-399.8. Authority to acquire historic properties.

When such action is reasonably necessary or appropriate for the preservation of a designated historic property, the commission may negotiate at any time with the owner for its preservation in accordance with the provisions of Parts 3A and 3B.

Appearance Commission

Municipal, County, or Joint

G.S. 160A-451.   Membership and appointment of commission; joint commission.

Each municipality and county in the State may create a special commission, to be known as the official appearance commission for the city or county. The commission shall consist of not less than seven nor more than 15 members, to be appointed by the governing body of the municipality or county for such terms, not to exceed four years, as the governing body may by ordinance provide. All members shall be residents of the municipality's or county's area of planning and zoning jurisdiction at the time of appointment. Where possible, appointments shall be made in such a manner as to maintain on the commission at all times a majority of members who have had special training or experience in a design field, such as architecture, landscape design, horticulture, city planning, or a closely related field. . . .

A county and one or more cities in the county may establish a joint appearance commission. If a joint commission is established, the county and the city or cities involved shall determine the residence requirements for members of the joint commission.

G.S. 160A-452.   Powers and duties of commission.

The commission, upon its appointment, shall make careful study of the visual problems and needs of the municipality or county within its area of zoning jurisdiction, and shall make any plans and carry out any programs that will, in accordance with the powers herein granted, enhance and improve the visual quality and aesthetic characteristics of the municipality or county. To this end, the governing board may confer upon the appearance commission the following powers and duties:

(1) To initiate, promote and assist in the implementation of programs of general community beautification in the municipality or county;

(2) To seek to coordinate the activities of individuals, agencies and organizations, public and private, whose plans, activities and programs bear upon the appearance of the municipality or county;

(3) To provide leadership and guidance in matters of area or community design and appearance to individuals, and to public and private organizations, and agencies;

(4) To make studies of the visual characteristics and problems of the municipality or county, including surveys and inventories of an appropriate nature, and to recommend standards and policies of design for the entire area, any portion or neighborhood thereof, or any project to be undertaken;

(5) To prepare both general and specific plans for the improved appearance of the municipality or county. These plans may include the entire area or any part thereof, and may include private as well as public property. The plans shall set forth desirable standards and goals for the aesthetic enhancement of the municipality or county or any part thereof within its area of planning and zoning jurisdiction, including public ways and areas, open spaces, and public and private buildings and projects;

(6) To participate, in any way deemed appropriate by the governing body of the municipality or county and specified in the ordinance establishing the commission, in the implementation of its plans. To this end, the governing body may include in the ordinance the following powers:

   a. To request from the proper officials of any public agency or body, including agencies of the State and its political subdivisions, its plans for public buildings, facilities, or projects to be located within the municipality or its area of planning and zoning jurisdiction of the city or county.

   b. To review these plans and to make recommendations regarding their aesthetic suitability to the appropriate agency, or to the municipal or county planning or governing board. . . .

   c. To formulate and recommend to the appropriate municipal planning or governing board the adoption or amendment of ordinances (including the zoning ordinance, subdivision regulations, and other local ordinances regulating the use of property) that will, in the opinion of the commission, serve to enhance the appearance of the municipality and its surrounding areas.

   d. To direct the attention of city or county officials to needed enforcement of any ordinance that may in any way affect the appearance of the city or county.

   e. To seek voluntary adherence to the standards and policies of its plans.

f. To enter, in the performance of its official duties and at reasonable times, upon private lands and make examinations or surveys.

g. To promote public interest in and an understanding of its recommendations, studies, and plans, and to that end to prepare, publish and distribute to the public such studies and reports as will, in the opinion of the commission, advance the cause of improved municipal or county appearance.

h. To conduct public meetings and hearings, giving reasonable notice to the public thereof.

G.S. 160A-453.   Staff services; advisory council.

The commission may recommend to the municipal or county governing board suitable arrangements for the procurement or provision of staff or technical services for the commission, and the governing board may appropriate such amount as it deems necessary to carry out the purposes for which it was created. The commission may establish an advisory council or other committees.

Inspection Department

Municipal or Joint

G.S. 160A-411.   Inspection department.

Every city in the State is hereby authorized to create an inspection department, and may appoint one or more inspectors who may be given the titles of building inspector, electrical inspector, plumbing inspector, housing inspector, zoning inspector, heating and air-conditioning inspector, fire prevention inspector, or deputy or assistant inspector, or such other titles as may be generally descriptive of the duties assigned. The department may be headed by a superintendent or director of inspections. Every city shall perform the duties and responsibilities set forth in G.S. 160A-412 either by: (i) creating its own inspection department; (ii) creating a joint inspection department in cooperation with one or more other units of local government . . . ; (iii) contracting with another unit of local government for the provision of inspection services . . . ; or (iv) arranging for the county in which it is located to perform inspection services within the city's jurisdiction . . . .

G.S. 160A-412.   Duties and responsibilities.

The duties and responsibilities of an inspection department and of the inspectors therein shall be to enforce within their territorial jurisdiction State and local laws relating to

(1) The construction of buildings and other structures;

(2) The installation of such facilities as plumbing systems, electrical systems, heating systems, refrigeration systems, and air-conditioning systems;

(3) The maintenance of buildings and other structures in a safe, sanitary, and healthful condition;

(4) Other matters that may be specified by the city council.

These duties shall include the receipt of applications for permits and the issuance or denial of permits, the making of any necessary inspections, the issuance or denial of certificates of compliance, the issuance of orders to correct violations, the bringing of judicial actions against actual or threatened violations, the keeping of adequate records, and any other actions that may be required in order adequately to enforce those laws. The city council shall have the authority to enact reasonable and appropriate provisions governing the enforcement of those laws.

G.S. 160A-413.   Joint inspection department; other arrangements.

A city council may enter into and carry out contracts with another city, county, or combination thereof under which the parties agree to create and support a joint inspection department for the enforcement of State and local laws specified in the agreement. The governing boards of the contracting parties are authorized to make any necessary appropriations for this purpose.

In lieu of a joint inspection department, a city council may designate an inspector from any other city or county to serve as a member of its inspection department with the approval of the governing body of the other city or county. The inspector shall, while exercising the duties of the position, be considered a municipal employee.

The city council of any city may request the board of county commissioners of the county in which the city is located to direct one or more county building inspectors to exercise their powers within part or all of the city's jurisdiction, and they shall thereupon be empowered to do so until the city council officially withdraws its request . . . .

County or Joint

G.S. 153A-351.   Inspection department; certification of electrical inspectors.

(a) A county may create an inspection department, consisting of one or more inspectors who may be given the titles of building inspector, electrical inspector, plumbing inspector, housing inspector, zoning inspector, heating and air-conditioning inspector, fire prevention inspector, deputy or assistant inspector, or any other title that is generally descriptive of the duties assigned. The department may be headed by a superintendent or director of inspections.

(a1) Every county shall perform the duties and responsibilities set forth in G.S. 153A-352 either by:

(1) Creating its own inspection department;

(2) Creating a joint inspection department in cooperation with one or more other units of local government . . . ; or,

(3) Contracting with another unit of local government for the provision of inspection services . . . .

G.S. 153A-352.   Duties and responsibilities.

The duties and responsibilities of an inspection department and of the inspectors in it are to enforce within the county's territorial jurisdiction State and local laws and local ordinances and regulations relating to:

(1) The construction of buildings;

(2) The installation of such facilities as plumbing systems, electrical systems, heating systems, refrigeration systems, and air-conditioning systems;

(3) The maintenance of buildings in a safe, sanitary, and healthful condition;

(4) Other matters that may be specified by the board of commissioners.

These duties and responsibilities include receiving applications for permits and issuing or denying permits, making necessary inspections, issuing or denying certificates of compliance, issuing orders to correct violations, bringing judicial actions against actual or threatened violations, keeping adequate records, and taking any other actions that may be required to adequately enforce the laws and ordinances and regulations. The board of commissioners may enact reasonable and appropriate provisions governing the enforcement of the laws and ordinances and regulations.

G.S. 153A-353.   Joint inspection department; other arrangements.

A county may enter into and carry out contracts with one or more other counties or cities under which the parties agree to create and support a joint inspection department for enforcing those State and local laws and local ordinances and regulations specified in the agreement. The governing bodies of the contracting units may make any necessary appropriations for this purpose.

In lieu of a joint inspection department, a county may designate an inspector from another county or from a city to serve as a member of the county inspection department, with the approval of the governing body of the other county or city. The inspector, while exercising the duties of the position, is a county employee.

Housing Code Enforcement

Municipal or County

G.S. 160A-442.   Definitions.

The following terms shall have the meanings whenever used or referred to as indicated when used in this Part unless a different meaning clearly appears from the context:

(1) "City" means any incorporated city or any county. . . .

(3) "Governing body" means the council, board of commissioners, or other legislative body, charged with governing a city or county. . . .

G.S. 160A-443.   Ordinance authorized as to repair, closing and demolition; order of public officer.

. . . the governing body of the city is hereby authorized to adopt and enforce ordinances relating to dwellings within the city's territorial jurisdiction that are unfit for human habitation. These ordinances shall include the following provisions:

(1) That a public officer be designated or appointed to exercise the powers prescribed by the ordinance.

(2) That whenever a petition is filed with the public officer . . . charging that any dwelling is unfit for human habitation or whenever it appears to the public officer (on his own motion) that any dwelling is unfit for human habitation, the public officer shall, if his preliminary investigation discloses a basis for such charges, issue and cause to be served upon the owner of and parties in interest in such dwellings a complaint stating the charges . . . and containing a notice that a hearing will be held before the public officer (or his designated agent) . . . .

(3) That if, after notice and hearing, the public officer determines that the dwelling under consideration is unfit for human habitation, he shall state in writing his findings of fact in support of that determination and shall issue and cause to be served upon the owner thereof an order,

    a. If the repair . . . can be made at a reasonable cost in relation to the value of the dwelling . . . , requiring the owner, within the time specified, to repair, alter or improve the dwelling in order to render it fit for human habitation or to vacate and close the dwelling as a human habitation; or

    b. If the repair . . . cannot be made at a reasonable cost in relation to the value of the dwelling . . . , requiring the owner, within the time specified in the order, to remove or demolish such dwelling.

(4) That, if the owner fails to comply with an order to repair, alter or improve or to vacate and close the dwelling, the public officer may cause the dwelling to be repaired, altered or improved or to be vacated and closed; ....

(5) That, if the owner fails to comply with an order to remove or demolish the dwelling, the public officer may cause such dwelling to be removed or demolished. The duties of the public officer set forth in subdivisions (4) and (5) shall not be exercised until the governing body shall have by ordinance ordered the public officer to proceed to effectuate the purpose of this Article with respect to the particular property or properties ....

(7) If any occupant fails to comply with an order to vacate a dwelling, the public officer may file a civil action in the name of the city to remove such occupant. ...

G.S. 160A-446.   Remedies.

(a) The governing body may provide for the creation and organization of a housing appeals board to which appeals may be taken from any decision or order of the public officer, or may provide for such appeals to be heard and determined by its zoning board of adjustment.

(b) The housing appeals board, if created, shall consist of five members to serve for three-year staggered terms. It shall have the power to elect its own officers, to fix the times and places for its meetings, to adopt necessary rules of procedure, and to adopt other rules and regulations for the proper discharge of its duties. ...

(c) An appeal from any decision or order of the public officer may be taken by any person aggrieved thereby or by any officer, board or commission of the city. ...

(d) The appeals board shall fix a reasonable time for hearing appeals, shall give due notice to the parties, and shall render its decision within a reasonable time. ... The board may reverse or affirm, wholly or partly, or may modify the decision or order appealed from, and may make any decision and order that in its opinion ought to be made in the matter, and to that end it shall have all the powers of the public officer .... The board shall have power also in passing upon appeals, when practical difficulties or unnecessary hardships would result from carrying out the strict letter of the ordinance, to adapt the application of the ordinance to the necessities of the case to the end that the spirit of the ordinance shall be observed, public safety and welfare secured, and substantial justice done.

(e) Every decision of the board shall be subject to review by proceedings in the nature of certiorari instituted within 15 days of the decision of the board, but not otherwise. ...

G.S. 160A-448.   Additional powers of public officer.

An ordinance adopted by the governing body of the city may authorize the public officer to exercise any powers necessary or convenient to carry out and effectuate the purpose and provisions of this Part, including the following powers in addition to others herein granted: . . .

(4)   To appoint and fix the duties of officers, agents and employees necessary to carry out the purposes of the ordinances; and

(5)   To delegate any of his functions and powers under the ordinance to other officers and other agents.

Community Development Programs

Municipal

G. S. 160A-456.   Community development programs and activities.

(a) Any city is authorized to engage in, to accept federal and State grants and loans for, and to appropriate and expend funds for community development programs and activities. In undertaking community development programs and activities, in addition to other authority granted by law, a city may engage in the following activities:

(1)   Programs of assistance and financing of rehabilitation of private buildings principally for the benefit of low and moderate income persons, or for the restoration or preservation of older neighborhoods or properties, including direct repair, the making of grants or loans, the subsidization of interest payments on loans, and the guaranty of loans;

(2)   Programs concerned with employment, economic development, crime prevention, child care, health, drug abuse, education, and welfare needs of persons of low and moderate income.

(b) Any city council may exercise directly those powers granted by law to municipal redevelopment commissions and those powers granted by law to municipal housing authorities, and may do so whether or not a redevelopment commission or housing authority is in existence in such city. Any city council desiring to do so may delegate to any redevelopment commission or to any housing authority the responsibility of undertaking or carrying out any specified community development activities. Any city council and any board of county commissioners may by agreement undertake or carry out for each other any specified community development activities. Any city council may contract with any person, association, or corporation in undertaking any specified community development activities. Any county or city board of health, county board of social services, or county or city board of education, may by agreement undertake or carry out for any city council any specified community development activities.

(c) Any city council undertaking community development programs or activities may create one or more advisory committees to advise it and to make recommendations concerning such programs or activities.

County

G.S. 153A-376.   Community development programs and activities.

(a) Any county is authorized to engage in, to accept federal and State grants and loans for, and to appropriate and expend funds for community development programs and activities. In undertaking community development programs and activities, in addition to other authority granted by law, a county may engage in the following activities:

(1) Programs of assistance and financing of rehabilitation of private buildings principally for the benefit of low and moderate income persons, or for the restoration or preservation of older neighborhoods or properties, including direct repair, the making of grants or loans, the subsidization of interest payments on loans, and the guaranty of loans;

(2) Programs concerned with employment, economic development, crime prevention, child care, health, drug abuse, education, and welfare needs of persons of low and moderate income.

(b) Any board of county commissioners may exercise directly those powers granted by law to county redevelopment commissions and those powers granted by law to county housing authorities. Any board of county commissioners desiring to do so may delegate to redevelopment commission or to any housing authority the responsibility of undertaking or carrying out any specified community development activities. Any board of county commissioners and any municipal governing body may by agreement undertake or carry out for each other any specified community development activities. Any board of county commissioners may contract with any person, association, or corporation in undertaking any specified community development activities. Any county or city board of health, county board of social services, or county or city board of education, may by agreement undertake or carry out for any board of county commissioners any specified community development activities.

(c) Any board of county commissioners undertaking community development programs or activities may create one or more advisory committees to advise it and to make recommendations concerning such programs or activities. . . .

Urban Renewal

Municipal, County, Regional, or Joint

G.S. 160A-503.   Definitions.

The following terms where used in this Article, shall have the following meanings, except where the context clearly indicates a different meaning: . . .

(9) "Municipality"—Any incorporated city or town, or any county. . . .

(15) "Redevelopment"—The acquisition, replanning, clearance, rehabilitation or rebuilding of an area for residential, recreational, commercial, industrial or other purposes, including the provision of streets, utilities, parks, recreational areas and other open spaces;   provided, without limiting the generality thereof, the term "redevelopment" may include a program of repair and rehabilitation of buildings and other improvements, and may include the exercise of any powers under this Article with respect to the area for which such program is undertaken.

(16) "Redevelopment area"—Any area which a planning commission may find to be

a. A blighted area . . . ;

b. A nonresidential redevelopment area . . . ;

c. A rehabilitation, conservation, and reconditioning area . . . ;

d. Any combination thereof, so as to require redevelopment under the provisions of this Article. . . .

(19) "Redevelopment project" shall mean any work or undertaking:

a. To acquire blighted or nonresidential redevelopment areas or portions thereof, or individual tracts in rehabilitation, conservation, and reconditioning areas, including lands, structures, or improvements, the acquisition of which is necessary or incidental to the proper clearance, development, or redevelopment of such areas or to the prevention of the spread or recurrence of conditions of blight;

b. To clear any such areas by demolition or removal of existing buildings, structures, streets, utilities or other improvements thereon and to install, construct, or reconstruct streets, utilities, and site improvements essential to the preparation of sites for uses in accordance with the redevelopment plan;

c. To sell land in such areas for residential, recreational, commercial, industrial or other use or for the public use to the highest bidder as herein set out or to retain such land for public use, in accordance with the redevelopment plan;

   d. To carry out plans for a program of voluntary or compulsory repair, rehabilitation, or reconditioning of buildings or other improvements in such areas . . . and

   e. To engage in programs of assistance and financing, including the making of loans, for rehabilitation, repair, construction, acquisition, or reconditioning of residential units and commercial and industrial facilities in a redevelopment area. . . .

G.S. 160A-504.   Formation of commissions.

(a) Each municipality, as defined herein, is hereby authorized to create separate and distinct bodies corporate and politic to be known as the redevelopment commission of the municipality by the passage by the governing body of such municipality of an ordinance or resolution creating a commission to function within the territorial limits of said municipality. . . .

G.S. 160A-505.   Alternative organization.

(a) In lieu of creating a redevelopment commission as authorized herein, the governing body of any municipality may, if it deems wise, either designate a housing authority . . . to exercise the powers, duties, and responsibilities of a redevelopment commission as prescribed herein, or undertake to exercise such powers, duties, and responsibilities itself. . . .

(b) The governing body of any municipality which has prior to July 1, 1969, created, or which may hereafter create, a redevelopment commission may, in its discretion, by resolution abolish such redevelopment commission . . . . Any municipality which abolishes a redevelopment commission pursuant to this subsection may, at any time subsequent to such abolition or concurrently therewith, exercise the authority granted by subsection (a) of this section.

. . . .

(c) Where the governing body of any municipality has in its discretion, by resolution, abolished a redevelopment commission pursuant to subsection (b) above, the governing body of such municipality may, at any time subsequent to the passage of a resolution abolishing a redevelopment commission, or concurrently therewith, . . . designate an existing housing authority . . . to exercise the powers, duties, and responsibilities of a redevelopment commission. . . .

G.S. 160A-506.   Creation of a county redevelopment commission.

If the board of county commissioners by resolution declares that blighted areas do exist in said county, and the redevelopment of such areas is necessary in the interest of public health, safety, morals, or welfare of the residents of such county, the county commissioners of said county are hereby authorized to create a separate and distinct body corporate and politic to be known as the redevelopment commission of said county . . . to function in the territorial limits of said county . . . .

G.S. 160A-507.   Creation of a regional redevelopment commission.

If the board of county commissioners of two or more contiguous counties by resolution declare that blighted areas do exist in said counties and the redevelopment of such areas is necessary in the interest of public health, morals, or welfare of residents of such counties, the county commissioners of said counties are hereby authorized to create a separate and distinct body corporate and politic to be known as the regional redevelopment commission by the passage of a resolution by each county to create such a commission to function in the territorial limits of the counties; . . . provided that the redevelopment commission shall not function in an area where such a commission exists or in the corporate limits of a municipality without resolution of agreement by the municipality.

G.S. 160A-507.1. Creation of a joint county-city redevelopment commission.

A county and one or more cities within the county are hereby authorized to create a separate and distinct body corporate and politic to be known as the joint redevelopment commission by the passage of a resolution by the board of county commissioners and the governing body of one or more cities within the county creating such a commission to function within the territorial limits of such participating units of government . . . .

G.S. 160A-513.   Preparation and adoption of redevelopment plans.

(a) A commission shall prepare a redevelopment plan for any area certified by the planning commission to be a redevelopment area. . . .

(b) The planning commission's certification of a redevelopment plan shall be made in conformance with its comprehensive general plan . . . for the area.

(c) A commission shall not acquire real property for a development project unless the governing body of the community in which the redevelopment project area is located has approved the redevelopment plan . . . .

(d) The redevelopment commission's redevelopment plan shall include, without being limited to, the following: . . .

(e) The commission shall hold a public hearing prior to its final determination of the redevelopment plan. . . .

(f) The commission shall submit the redevelopment plan to the planning commission for review. . . .

(g) Upon receipt of the planning commission's recommendation, . . . the commission shall submit to the governing body the redevelopment plan with the recommendation, if any, of the planning commission thereon. . . .

(h) The governing body, upon receipt of the redevelopment plan and the recommendations (if any) of the planning commission, shall hold a public hearing upon said plan. . . .

(i) The governing body shall approve, amend, or reject the redevelopment plan as submitted.

(j) . . . upon approval by the governing body of the redevelopment plan, the commission is authorized to acquire property, to execute contracts for clearance and preparation of the land for resale, and to take other actions necessary to carry out the plan . . . .

(k) A redevelopment plan may be modified at any time by the commission; provided that, if modified after the sale of real property in the redevelopment project area, the modification must be consented to by the redeveloper of such real property or his successor, or their successors in interest affected by the proposed modification. Where the proposed modification will substantially change the redevelopment plan as previously approved by the governing body the modification must similarly be approved by the governing body as provided above.

Housing Authority

Municipal, County, Regional, or Consolidated

G.S. 157-4.   Notice, hearing and creation of authority; cancellation of certificate of incorporation.

Any 25 residents of a city and of the area within 10 miles from the territorial boundaries thereof may file a petition with the city clerk setting forth that there is a need for an authority to function in the city and said surrounding area. . . .

. . . After . . . a hearing, the council shall determine:

(1) Whether insanitary or unsafe inhabited dwelling accommodations exist in the city and said surrounding area, and/or

(2) Whether there is a lack of safe or sanitary dwelling accommodations in the city and said surrounding area available for all the inhabitants thereof. . . .

If it shall determine that either or both of the above enumerated conditions exist, the council shall adopt a resolution so finding . . . and shall cause notice of such determination to be given to the mayor who shall thereupon appoint . . . not less than five nor more than nine commissioners to act as an authority. . . . [After an application to the Secretary of State for incorporation has been approved, he may issue a certificate of incorporation for the authority.]

G.S. 157-4.1.   Alternative organization.

(a) In lieu of creating a housing authority as authorized herein, the council of any city may, if it deems wise, either designate a redevelopment commission . . . to exercise the powers, duties, and responsibilities of a housing authority as prescribed herein, or may itself exercise such powers, duties, and responsibilities. . . .

(b) The council of any city which has prior to July 1, 1969, created, or which may hereafter create, a housing authority may, in its discretion, by resolution abolish such housing authority . . . . Upon the adoption of such a resolution, the housing authority of the city is hereby authorized and directed to take such actions . . . as will effectively transfer its authority, responsibilities, obligations, personnel, and property . . . to the city. Any city which abolishes a housing authority pursuant to this subsection may . . . exercise the authority granted by subsection (a) of this section.

.   .   .   .

(c) Where the governing body of any municipality has . . . by resolution abolished a housing authority, pursuant to subsection (b) above, the governing body . . . may . . . designate an existing redevelopment commission . . . to exercise the powers, duties, and responsibilities of a housing authority. . . .

G.S. 157-33.   Notice, hearing and creation of authority for a county.

Any 25 residents of a county may file a petition with the clerk of the board of county commissioners setting forth that there is a need for an authority to function in the county. . . .

. . . After . . . a hearing, the board of county commissioners shall determine (i) whether unsanitary or unsafe inhabited dwelling accommodations exist in the county and/or (ii) whether there is a lack of safe or sanitary dwelling accommodations in the county available for all the inhabitants thereof. . . .

If it shall determine that either or both of the above enumerated conditions exist, the board of county commissioners shall adopt a resolution so finding . . . and shall thereupon either (i) determine that the board of county commissioners shall itself constitute and act ex officio as an authority or (ii) appoint, as hereinafter provided, not less than five nor more than nine commissioners to act as an authority. . . . [After an application to the Secretary of State for incorporation has been approved, he may issue a certificate of incorporation for the authority.]

G.S. 157-35.   Creation of regional housing authority.

If the board of county commissioners of each of two or more contiguous counties having an aggregate population of more than 60,000 by resolution declares that there is a need for one housing authority to be created for all of such counties . . . a public body corporate and politic to be known as a regional housing authority for all of such counties shall . . . thereupon exist for and exercise its powers and other functions in such counties; and thereupon any housing authority created for any of such counties shall cease to exist except for the purpose of winding up its affairs and executing a deed to the regional housing authority as hereinafter provided . . . .

G.S. 157-39.5.   Consolidated housing authority.

If the governing body of each of two or more municipalities (with a population of less than 500, but having an aggregate population of more than 500) by resolution declares that there is a need for one housing authority for all of such municipalities to exercise in such municipalities the powers and other functions prescribed for a housing authority, a public body corporate and politic to be known as a consolidated housing authority . . . shall thereupon exist for all of such municipalities . . . and thereupon any housing authority created for any of such municipalities shall cease to exist except for the purpose of winding up its affairs and executing a deed of its real property to the consolidated housing authority . . . .

G.S. 157-39.1.   Area of operation of city, county and regional housing authorities.

(a) The boundaries or area of operation of a housing authority created for a city shall include said city and the area within 10 miles from the territorial boundaries of said city, but in no event shall it include the whole or a part of any other city, except as otherwise provided herein. . . . The area of operation or boundaries of a housing authority created for a county shall include all of the county for which it is created and the area of operation or boundaries of a regional housing authority shall include . . . all of the counties for which such regional housing authority is created and established: Provided, that a county or regional housing authority shall not undertake any housing project or projects within the boundaries of any city unless a resolution shall have been adopted by the governing body of such city (and also by any housing authority which shall have been theretofore established . . . to exercise its powers in such city) declaring that there is a need for the county or regional housing authority to exercise its power within such city . . . .

Economic Development

Municipal, County, or Regional

G.S. 158-8.　　**Creation of municipal, county or regional commissions authorized; composition; joining or withdrawing from regional commissions.**

The governing body of any municipality or the board of county commissioners of any county may by resolution create an economic development commission for said municipality or county. The governing bodies of any two or more municipalities and/or counties may by joint resolution, adopted by separate vote of each governing body concerned, create a regional economic development commission. . . .

G.S. 158-13.　　**Powers and duties.**

Any economic development commission created pursuant to this Article shall:

(1) Receive from any municipal, county, joint, or regional planning board or commission with jurisdiction within its area an economic development program for part or all of the area;

(2) Formulate projects for carrying out such economic development program . . . .

G.S. 158-14.　　**Regional planning and economic development commissions authorized.**

Any municipalities and/or counties desiring to exercise the powers granted by this Article may, at their option, create a regional planning and economic development commission, which shall have and exercise all of the powers and duties granted to a regional economic development commission under this Article and in addition the powers and duties granted to a regional planning commission under Article 23 of Chapter 153. . . .

G.S. 158-21.　　**Creation of industrial development commission; membership and terms of office; vacancies; meetings; selection of officers; bylaws and procedural rules and policies; authority of treasurer and required bond; subsidy or investment in business or industry forbidden.**

If the majority of the qualified voters voting in such election favor the levying of such a tax, then and in that event, the county commissioners may create a commission to be known as the "Industrial Development Commission" for said county. . . .

G.S. 158-23.   Board of county commissioners may function and carry out duties of industrial development commission.

Nothing herein shall prevent the board of county commissioners itself from functioning and carrying out the duties of the industrial development commission as provided for herein.

[G.S. 158-24 specifies 21 counties to which the article containing the two sections just excerpted applies.]

G.S. 159C-4.   Creation of authorities.

(a) The governing body of any county is hereby authorized to create by resolution a political subdivision and body corporate and politic of the State known as "The . . . County Industrial Facilities and Pollution Control Financing Authority" . . . .

[This chapter of the General Statutes then authorizes the Authority to issue bonds for and acquire or develop industrial sites and facilities for transfer to industries.]

3

Major Elements and Common Functions of Local Planning Organizations

As Chapter 2 indicates, the North Carolina General Assembly has been lavish in its grants of authority to local governments to create whatever local planning organizations they desire. Indeed, this generosity overwhelms many local units; they are more confused than enlightened by the feast of alternatives placed before them. To aid their understanding, this chapter lists some of the major organizational entities and briefly describes the functions of each one. Chapters 4 through 7 consider four traditional elements of local planning organizations, to present a better view of their roles and functions.

Governing Board
(City Council or Board of County Commissioners)

Primary responsibilities: legislative (G.S. Ch. 160A; G.S. Ch. 153A): adopts policies, ordinances, amendments; appropriates funds; approves acquisition, construction, and disposition of public facilities; oversees administration.

Possible secondary responsibilities: quasi-judicial and *administrative:* may issue special- or conditional-use permits under zoning ordinance (G.S. 160A-381; 153A-340); may approve subdivision plats (G.S. 160A-373; 153A-332); must approve redevelopment plans (G.S. 160A-513).

Authority to serve as other agencies: planning agency (G.S. 160A-361; 153A-321); *redevelopment commission* (G.S. 160A-456, 160A-505; 153A-376); *housing authority* (G.S. 160A-456, 157-4.1; 153A-376, 157-34).

Planning Board or Planning Commission
(G.S. 160A-361; 153A-321. May have some similar title)

Primary responsibilities: advisory: works with planning staff in making studies and developing policies, plans, and ordinances (G.S.

160A-361; 153A-321); prepares zoning ordinance and certifies it to governing board for adoption (G.S. 160A-387; 153A-344); makes recommandations to governing board concerning proposed zoning amendments (G.S. 153A-344); advises governing board on other matters as requested or directed.

Possible secondary responsibilities: administrative or *advisory:* approves, or makes recommendations to governing board concerning, proposed subdivision plats (G.S. 160A-373; 153A-332); certifies redevelopment areas and makes recommendations concerning redevelopment plans (G.S. 160A-513); prepares economic development program (G.S. 158-13).

Authority to serve as other agencies: historic district commission (G.S. 160A-396); *historic properties commission* (G.S. 160A-399.2); *zoning board of adjustment* (G.S. 160A-388; 153A-345).

Planning Department
(G.S. 160A-361, 160A-363; 153A-321, 153A-322)

Primary responsibilities: staff: makes studies; with planning board develops plans, policies, ordinances; advises manager, department heads, planning board, governing board on planning matters.

Possible secondary responsibilities: operational: develops and carries out community development programs, economic development programs, and building and housing inspection programs.

Department of Community Development
(G.S. Ch. 160A, Art. 19, Part 8; Ch. 153A, Art. 18, Part 5)

Primary responsibilities: operational: develops and carries out community development programs.

Possible secondary responsibilities: operational: administers inspection and planning staffs.

Inspection Department
(G.S. 160A-411; 153A-351)

Primary responsibilities: operational: enforces State Building Code and other state and local laws relating to construction (G.S. 160A-412; 153A-352).

Possible secondary responsibilities: operational: enforces minimum-housing-standards ordinance, zoning ordinance, sign ordinance, and other ordinances as assigned by governing board and manager.

Zoning Board of Adjustment
(G.S. 160A-388; 153A-345)

Primary responsibilities: quasi-judicial: hears appeals from zoning enforcement officer, grants special-use permits and variances (G.S. 160A-381, 160A-388; 153A-340, 153A-345).

Authority to serve as other agencies: housing appeals board (G.S. 160A-446); *airport zoning board of appeals* (G.S. 63-33).

Housing Appeals Board
(G.S. 160A-446)

Primary responsibilities: quasi-judicial: hears appeals under minimum-housing-standards ordinance (G.S. 160A-446).

Airport Zoning Board of Appeals
(G.S. 63-33)

Primary responsibilities: quasi-judicial: hears appeals under airport zoning ordinance (G.S. 63-33).

Historic District Commission
(G.S. 160A-396)

Primary responsibilities: quasi-judicial: issues certificates of appropriateness for changes in appearance of structures in historic districts (G.S. 160A-397); seeks alternative uses for buildings proposed for demolition in historic districts (G.S. 160A-399).

Authority to serve as other agencies: historic properties commission (G.S. 160A-399.2).

Historic Properties Commission
(G.S. 160A-399.1)

Primary responsibilities: advisory and *quasi-judicial:* recommends to governing board properties to be designated historic properties, acquires and manages historic properties, conducts educational programs (G.S. 160A-399.4); issues certificates of appropriateness for changes in appearance of historic properties (G.S. 160A-399.6); seeks alternative uses for historic properties proposed for demolition (G.S. 160A-399.6).

Authority to serve as other agencies: historic district commission (G.S. 160A-396).

Appearance Commission
(G.S. 160A-451)

Primary responsibilities: promotional: develops voluntary programs, policies, plans, and ordinances to improve community appearance; advises governmental agencies on aesthetic matters.

Authority to serve as other agencies: historic district commission (G.S. 160A-396).

Redevelopment Commission
(G.S. 160A-504; 160A-506)

Primary responsibilities: operational: develops and carries out redevelopment projects (G.S. Ch. 160A, Art. 22).

Possible secondary responsibilities: operational: operates community development programs (G.S. 160A-456, 153A-376).

Authority to serve as other agencies: housing authority (G.S. 157-4.1).

Housing Authority
(G.S. 157-4, 157-33)

Primary responsibilities: operational: develops, carries out, and operates public housing programs and projects (G.S. Ch. 157).

Possible secondary responsibilities: operational: operates community development programs (G.S. 160A-456, 153A-376).

Authority to serve as other agencies: redevelopment commission (G.S. 160A-505).

Economic Development Commission
(G.S. 158-8, 158-10)

Primary responsibilities: operational: formulates economic development projects and promotes economic development of area (G.S. 158-13).

Some of the entities just listed are mandatory elements of particular programs. If the local government elects not to embark upon a certain program, no organizational entity is required to operate that program; but if it chooses to have such a program, it must organize in the prescribed manner. With respect to most programs, however, the local governing board and administrator have options under the statutes to use one or another organizational approach. In some cases the statutes give the governing body almost complete freedom to "hand-craft" the organization to suit its needs, personnel and other resources, and desires.

4

The Governing Board

Although it may be foolish to single out any one element of a local planning organization as the most important, the key to success of any planning program is the local governing board. This is because the whole purpose of a planning organization is to provide advice and assistance to the governing board as it carries out its policy-making duties. If the governing board chooses to ignore this advice and assistance, or if it financially starves the planning organization to such an extent that the advice produced is ill-informed and unreliable, it would do better to save the taxpayers' money by dropping the whole operation. There is no justification for maintaining this elaborate organization just so that the governing board can preserve a public image of a forward-thinking local government.

The production of plans per se is not the objective of a planning program. Rather, the objective is the production of studies and plans that can furnish some guidance to the policy makers and the administrators as they carry out their duties. Without agreed-upon goals and comprehensive programs for attaining the goals, the operations of any local government are apt to be uncoordinated (possibly even conflicting), inefficient, and wasteful.

Planning is an attitude and an approach—an effort to agree upon goals and programs in a rational way, in advance of the need for decisions on particular matters. The governing board that chooses this approach may avoid many of the headaches and the frustrations attendant upon ad hoc decision making with no guidelines other than hasty analysis of political pros and cons. However, unless it really follows through and uses the guidelines that are developed in the planning process, a lot of effort and money will have been expended to no purpose.

This does not mean that the governing board must always accept the advice of its planning board—particularly if that advice itself is ad hoc and not based upon rational studies and plans. The governing board, by its nature, must take into account other factors than those considered by the planning agencies, and occasionally this will lead to decisions diametrically opposed to the planning agencies' recommendations. When that happens, the governing board should be aware that it is going counter to earlier plans and have good reasons for doing so.

Functions of the Governing Board

The governing board's role in planning begins with the creation of the planning organization. It continues with the process of making financial and other support available to the planning organization. It may involve the adoption of certain plans as official statements of policy. Finally, it includes the taking and the supervision of actions to carry out plans.

Tooling Up

Under the General Statutes local governing boards are authorized to create planning boards or planning commissions; appoint their members; and provide them with staff assistance, financial support, a place to meet, and other services and facilities. This authority is found in the following enabling acts (excerpts from which are set forth in Chapter 2):

Municipal planning board: G.S. 160A-146; 160A-361.

County planning board: G.S. 153A-76; 153A-321.

Joint planning board (municipalities, counties, or mixed): G.S. 160A-361; 153A-321; G.S. Ch. 160A, Art. 20, Part 1.

Regional planning commission: G.S. Ch. 153A, Art. 19.

Regional planning and economic development commission: G.S. 153A-398.

Regional council of governments: G.S. Ch. 160A, Art. 20.

The full text of these acts can be found in the current edition of the Institute of Government's publication, *Planning Legislation in North Carolina.*

Creating a Planning Board

Creating a planning board normally involves either the adoption of an *ordinance* (in the case of a municipal or county planning board) or the making of an *agreement* between two or more units (in the case of a joint planning board, a regional planning commission, a regional planning and economic development commission, or a regional council of governments). Sample copies of such ordinances and agreements are set forth in the appendixes to this book. In some cases, however, agencies have been created by *acts of the General Assembly* applying either to a particular unit (as a part of its charter) or to a regional organization.

The governing board should be aware that it is not limited to one of these types of planning agencies. Every local government in the state is part of a governmental region normally served by either a regional planning and economic development commission or a regional council of governments. In addition, many units are part of more limited regions consisting of a few cities and counties with special ties or interests. Governments that are members of such organizations commonly retain their individual planning organizations as well.

Appointing Board Members

The ordinance or the agreement that creates a planning board should specify the membership (for city and county planning boards this cannot be fewer than three), terms, qualifications, and compensation (if any) of the board. Normally members will be appointed by the governing board(s) of the unit(s) creating the planning board. If the board serves a municipality exercising extraterritorial jurisdiction under G.S. 160A-360, there must be at least one member (appointed by the board of county commissioners) who is a resident of the extraterritorial area.

In appointing members the board should be aware of two constitutional provisions that apply to officers. These are the so-called double-office-holding prohibition of Article VI, Section 9, and the provisions of Article VI, Section 8, which set forth several grounds of disqualification for office. It is uncertain whether membership on a planning board constitutes an office, but to the degree that the planning board is given decision-making responsibilities (rather than purely advisory ones), assuming that membership does constitute an office is prudent. Article VI, Section 9, reads as follows:

> **Dual office holding.**
>
> (1) *Prohibitions.* It is salutary that the responsibilities of self-government be widely shared among the citizens of the State and that the potential abuse of authority inherent in the holding of multiple offices by an individual be avoided. Therefore, no person who holds any office or place of trust or profit under the United States or any department

thereof, or under any other state or government, shall be eligible to hold any office in this State that is filled by election by the people. No person shall hold concurrently any two or more appointive offices or places of trust or profit, or any combination of elective and appointive offices or places of trust or profit, except as the General Assembly shall provide by general law.

(2) *Exceptions.* The provisions of this Section shall not prohibit any officer of the military forces of the State or of the United States not on active duty for an extensive period of time, any notary public, or any delegate to a Convention of the People from holding concurrently another office or place of trust or profit under this State or the United States or any department thereof.

The statutes effectuating these provisions are as follows:

G.S.128-1. No person shall hold more than one office; exception.

No person who shall hold any office or place of trust or profit under the United States, or any department thereof or under this State, or under any other state or government, shall hold or exercise any other office or place of trust or profit under the authority of this State, or be eligible to a seat in either house of the General Assembly except as provided in G.S. 128-1.1.

G.S. 128-1.1. Dual-office holding allowed.

(a) Any person who holds an appointive office, place of trust or profit in State or local government is hereby authorized by the General Assembly, pursuant to Article VI, Sec. 9 of the North Carolina Constitution, to hold concurrently one other appointive office, place of trust or profit, or an elective office in either State or local government.

(b) Any person who holds an elective office in State or local government is hereby authorized by the General Assembly, pursuant to Article VI, Sec. 9 of the North Carolina Constitution, to hold concurrently one other appointive office, place of trust or profit, in either State or local government.

(c) Any person who holds an office or position in the federal postal system is hereby authorized to hold concurrently therewith one position in State or local government.

(d) The term "elective office," as used herein, shall mean any office filled by election by the people when the election is conducted by a county or municipal board of elections under the supervision of the State Board of Elections.

G.S. 128-2. Holding office contrary to the Constitution; penalty.

If any person presumes to hold any office, or place of trust or profit, or is elected to a seat in either house of the General Assembly, contrary to Article VI, Sec. 9 of the North Carolina Constitution, he shall forfeit all rights and emoluments incident thereto.

Thus no one should accept appointment to the planning board (if it is construed to be an office) if he or she holds more than one other elective or appointive office. A person who does so may forfeit one (and perhaps all) of his or her offices.

On the other hand, the North Carolina Supreme Court has held that when a statute or an ordinance provides that the holder of one office will *automatically* be the holder of another (this is commonly referred to as ex officio membership in the second position), there is no dual-office holding. Instead, the Court says that this merely amounts to imposition of additional duties on the holder of the first office.

Article VI, Section 8, reads as follows:

> **Disqualifications for office.**
> The following persons shall be disqualified for office:
> First, any person who shall deny the being of Almighty God.
> Second, with respect to any office that is filled by election by the people, any person who is not qualified to vote in an election for that office.
> Third, any person who has been adjudged guilty of treason or any other felony against this State or the United States, or any person who has been adjudged guilty of a felony in another state that also would be a felony if it had been committed in this State, or any person who has been adjudged guilty of corruption or malpractice in any office, and who has not been restored to the rights of citizenship in the manner prescribed by law.

Apart from these legal restraints (and any that might have been imposed by its charter), the governing board is relatively free to select as members those whom it considers best qualified. In doing so, it should give serious consideration to *why* it wants a board: to have a sounding board of citizens of the community? to obtain the advice of people whom it considers uniquely qualified by training or experience? to secure some free professional advice? to provide a training ground for future leaders of the community? to hear from representatives of organizations or neighborhoods?

Perhaps the best approach that the governing board can use in answering such questions is to remember that it is selecting advisors to itself. This means that it should appoint people whose views and judgments it will respect—and perhaps some representatives of groups in the community who do not normally have a voice in decisions.

Among the qualities that it may feel are particularly important are (a) balanced judgment and judicious temperament; (b) imagination and intelligence; (c) an understanding of the development process and its costs; (d) willingness to take a stand without becoming unduly stubborn; (e) contacts with, and the confidence of, a broad cross-section of citizens; (f) an absence of major conflicts of interest; (g) recognition that an adviser is not entitled to expect the advice offered to be followed 100 percent of the time; and (h) tolerance of opposing views.

Although the statutes (G.S. 160A-363; 153A-322) specifically authorize payment of compensation to planning board members, most serve without pay. In some cases a small payment is made for attendance at each meeting, as a means of encouraging members to attend. Ordinarily, planning board members are reimbursed for out-of-pocket expenditures incurred in performing their duties; provision for such reimbursement should be included in the ordinance or agreement establishing the board and in the annual budget. Boards whose members must travel some distance to meetings are particularly likely to appreciate this type of reimbursement.

The governing board should also give some attention to the terms of the members. Because effective work on a planning board requires a certain amount of technical knowledge, new board members must spend some time educating themselves as to functions and procedures. To avoid the necessity (and consequent time involved) of educating an entirely new board at periodic intervals, it is common for the ordinance to provide for staggered terms. These are ordinarily created by appointing the initial members to different terms and their successors to uniform terms (e.g., initial members of a three-person board might be appointed for one-, two-, and three-year terms, and their successors, for three-year terms).

It has been suggested that there is merit in injecting new blood into a board's membership periodically. This may occur naturally, as a result of members' desires not to be reappointed. It may also be done by limiting members to a stated number of terms. Such a limitation might be imposed by an ordinance provision, by the board's rules of procedures, or merely by an unstated policy.

Providing Support Staff

To be effective, a planning board must have adequate support services. Unlike some other boards and commissions that require only secretarial services, the planning board usually needs technical assistance. This may be furnished from a variety of sources:

1. A full-time planning staff hired by the governmental unit.
2. A private planning consultant hired to assist the planning board and its staff (a consultant may be hired to provide specialized services even when there is a full-time staff).

3. The staff of another planning board whose services are contracted for (under G.S. Ch. 160A, Art. 20, Part 1).
4. The staff of a regional council of governments (under G.S. Ch. 160A, Art. 20, Part 2).
5. The staff of a regional planning commission or a regional planning and economic development commission (under G.S. Ch. 153A, Art. 19).
6. The staff of the North Carolina Department of Natural Resources and Community Development (usually made available through its regional offices).
7. The city or county attorney or a specially hired attorney, part-time or full-time.
8. Other local governmental employees, such as an assistant manager, an engineer, or a building inspector.
9. Volunteer workers, such as civic club members, college and high school students, or Boy Scouts and Girl Scouts.

Which of these approaches is the most satisfactory for a particular local government will depend upon such factors as its financial status, its size, and the availability of professional planners. In general, there is such a shortage of professional planners in comparison with the demand for their services that few of the smaller units can afford a full-time planner. These units will do best in most cases to contract for professional services from the Department of Natural Resources and Community Development, regional organizations, larger units in the area, or private planning consultants, and provide local personnel to do the routine jobs that are required.

Participating in Plan Preparation and Adoption

There is no legal requirement that the governing board participate in any manner in the process of plan making, nor under the North Carolina statutes must it adopt any plans other than a major street plan (jointly adopted by the board and the Department of Transportation, under G.S. Ch. 136, Art. 3A). However, if (as indicated earlier) the objective of planning is to produce informed advice for the governing board from the planning board, it seems natural for the governing board to take an interest in the thoroughness with which the planning board makes the studies and the plans on which advice will be based. This means that the governing board should at a minimum require periodic reports from the planning board concerning its activities. Ideally one or more of the governing board members would routinely attend planning board meetings; minutes of board meetings would be exchanged; as studies and plans were completed, the governing board would ask the planning board to brief it on details; and the two boards would meet informally from time to time to consider common problems. Many local units provide for jointly conducted public hearings by the two boards on proposals for zoning amendments. There may be other occasions on which a joint hearing would be desirable.

If adopted, the plan may become a basis for decisions on proposed zoning amendments, proposed subdivisions, and the nature and the contents of redevelopment projects. It may also have important impacts on location of major thoroughfares, parks and playgrounds, civic centers, water and sewage treatment plants, schools, and other facilities. Some units have policies that whenever the planning board makes a recommendation with regard to any of the above matters, it begin by noting whether the proposal is in accord with the plan (and if not, how the plan should be modified to reflect the proposed action).

If the plan is to have this importance, the governing board might well adopt it formally. Adoption would have the dual purposes of (a) encouraging board members to familiarize themselves with the contents of the plan, so that they would more readily refer to it in the future, and (b) announcing to property owners and other developers the local government's intentions as to how various areas should develop, so that they could do their own planning in accordance with its proposals.

There is no prescribed procedure for such adoption. If the board wishes, it can hold one or more public hearings before it acts, but this is not required by statute. Presumably the actual instrument of adoption should be a board resolution, rather than an ordinance. In any event, if the plan is adopted, consideration should be given to publication, so that the public at large may become familiar with it.

Carrying Out Plans

Normally if a plan is to be transformed from paper into reality, there must be (a) appropriations of public funds to acquire land and build facilities for public use and (b) regulations for private development and use of land. Under the law, only the local governing board can take such actions, although it may call upon various officials and agencies to assist it.

Appropriations

Most plans call for provision of a range of public facilities, such as libraries, schools, museums, a city hall or a courthouse, fire stations, streets, water storage and pumping facilities, sewage treatment plants, playgrounds, and other recreation areas. Some of these facilities represent mere provision of routine governmental services to newly developed areas. Others reflect a deliberate effort to upgrade the existing environment.

Although governing boards are accustomed to making appropriations for such facilities, they do not always realize the full benefits that could be derived from the appropriations because they do not consciously use the location of new facilities to influence the pattern of private development. Construction of a school, a golf course, or a major thoroughfare in a particular area may attract new residential or other development. Conversely, building a new sewage treatment plant, a jail, or a crowd-drawing facility such as an athletic stadium in an area might well discourage nearby residential development, but encourage other forms of growth. The provision or denial of facilities for water and sewerage service in a particular area may have a considerable impact on its development; some cities have announced schedules showing the sequence in which they will extend water and sewerage service to various areas, thus encouraging growth to take place in the same sequence.

To ensure that consideration is given to possibilities for using public improvements to influence the pattern of development, and to prevent inconsistent planning by different departments, two administrative devices are commonly used. One is to require (by ordinance or administrative directive) that proposed public facilities be referred to the planning staff or the planning board for its recommendations, preferably before detailed project plans are begun. The second is to mandate that all public projects be included in a comprehensive capital improvements program in whose preparation the planning officials play a part (this is described at greater length in Chapter 5).

Regardless of whether such devices are used by their local government, governing board members should always ask themselves before voting on an appropriation for a public improvement, How does this fit into our plan? Could we have more impact on private development if we built it at a different location or at a different time? Will this be adequate in size to meet the needs forecast under our plan? Will its location conflict with proposals of other agencies?

Regulatory Ordinances

To ensure that private development takes place in the pattern that is intended and at the densities for which public facilities have been planned, legal regulations must be adopted. As the local legislative body, the governing board has this responsibility.

It may adopt *subdivision regulations* governing the conversion of raw land into building sites served by streets, water and sewerage systems, and other supporting facilities, under the provisions of G.S. Chapter 160A, Article 19, Part 2 (municipal) or G.S. Chapter 153A, Article 18, Part 2 (county). Further, it may assign responsibility for enforcement of such regulations to itself, to a planning board, to its planning staff, to a committee of technically trained people, or even to an individual (such as the city engineer).

It may adopt a *zoning ordinance* controlling the type and the intensity of development in various areas (zones) of its jurisdiction, under provisions of G.S. Chapter 160A, Article 19, Part 3 (municipal) or G.S. Chapter 153A, Article 18, Part 3 (county). It may assign initial enforcement of this ordinance to a zoning administrator or a building inspector. It may delegate responsibility for hearing appeals from that official's decisions and for granting relief in hardship situations (variances) to a board of adjustment. It may assign responsibility for granting special permits (variously called special-use permits, conditional-use permits, or exceptions) to itself, to the board of adjustment, or to the planning board.

If it wishes to protect special *historic districts,* it may do so under its zoning ordinance and additional powers granted by G.S. Chapter 160A, Article 19, Part 3A. In addition to usual zoning officials, it may create a historic district commission to enforce these provisions. If instead it wishes merely to protect individual *historic properties,* it may create a historic properties commission under G.S. Chapter 160A, Article 19, Part 3B.

In general, the state exercises control over construction through the *State Building Code* adopted by the Building Code Council under provisions of G.S. Chapter 143, Article 9. However, local governments have responsibility for enforcement of this code through local inspectors appointed under G.S. Chapter 160A, Article 19, Part 5 (municipal) or G.S. Chapter 153A, Article 18, Part 4 (county).

The governing board may adopt a *housing code* under G.S. Chapter 160A, Article 19, Part 6, and it may appoint inspectors to enforce this code. If it wishes to establish a broader program to deal with housing problems, it may do so with its *community development* powers under

G.S. Chapter 160A, Article 19, Part 8 (municipal) or G.S. Chapter 153A, Article 18, Part 5 (county). Or it may establish a *housing authority* under G.S. Chapter 157 or a *redevelopment commission* under G.S. Chapter 160A, Article 22.

Alternatively the governing board may decide to push for economic development. If so, it may create an *economic development commission* under G.S. Chapter 158, Article 2 or 3.

These are only some of the more elaborate options the governing board has when it seeks to influence patterns of private development. Further, through its general ordinance-making powers, it can attack a multiplicity of problems with individual ordinances (such as a sign ordinance, a junked-car ordinance, a mobile-home-park ordinance, a skateboard ordinance, or an ordinance addressing whatever is perceived as a problem in the unit).

Adoption of Policies Furthering Plan Objectives

Most of the preceding options are regulatory in their impact. The governing board has yet another tool at its disposal: *policies* with respect to assessments, extension of utilities, cost-sharing for various improvements, and so forth. For example, policies that sharply increase the cost of utilities connections for development beyond the city limits will encourage a pattern of compact, close-in development, resulting in requests for (rather than opposition to) annexation. Requirement of heavier pavement, more costly curbs and gutters, and larger utilities mains in areas of high-density development may influence developers to reduce such density when they believe land costs are less than extra improvement costs. Such policies may do little to reduce the rate of development when pressures are intense, but through required impact fees and related provisions, the city may place more of the cost of new development on the property owners benefited than on the population at large.

What all of the foregoing suggests is that the governing board has a great range of tools through which it can operate. It is uniquely authorized to play a leading role in carrying out whatever plans and policies it determines to be best for its unit.

5

The Planning Board

As previous chapters have indicated, North Carolina statutes permit, and local governments have created, many varieties of citizen boards as part of the planning structure. This chapter focuses on the most common variety—the planning board or planning commission.

Origin and Role of the Planning Board

The planning board as part of the local planning organization in America is explainable mostly in historical terms. In other countries it is usual for a local governing board to exercise its functions without the advice of a separate citizen board. Such administrative functions as the usual American planning board performs are handled either by the governing board itself or by full-time administrative officials.

The concept of the separate planning board grew out of the muckraking period in America, that time around the turn of the century when reporters were busily exposing corruption in municipal governments and reformers were busily attempting to remove power from the politicians who had abused it. One tack that was taken was to professionalize the administration of local government, this resulting in the city manager form of government. Another was to place responsibility for particular functions in the hands of citizen boards separate from the governing boards, this leading on the one hand to separate school boards and on the other to separate planning boards.

Such lawyers as Alfred Bettman of Cincinnati and Edward Bassett of New York, who drafted most of America's early planning laws, were members of the reform movement, and their influence was strongly felt in the organizational structure that evolved. Both Bettman and Bassett were members of the Advisory Committee on City Planning and Zoning of the U.S. Department of Commerce (appointed by Secretary Herbert Hoover), which produced *A Standard State Zoning Enabling Act*[1] and *A Standard City Planning Enabling Act,*[2] the models from which most present-day planning legislation stems.

In the annotations to the *Standard City Planning Enabling Act* are to be found such revealing statements as the following:

> Planning is just as important and essential a function of city government as is administration or legislation. In other words, the successful and efficient work of city government, for the promotion of the public health, convenience, safety, and welfare, requires the exercise of the three distinct functions of planning, legislation, and administration, each in charge of separate officers or boards. The planning board is that organ of the municipal government which performs this planning function, and within its sphere it needs the same independence, specialized qualification, and permanence as the other organs of the city government need in their respective spheres.[3]

> As stated, the planning function is quite separate and distinct from the legislative function. The city council represents the people of the city for the length of the term for which it is elected and during that term is to be deemed to possess the qualifications for and has its time and energies taken up with the problems of current legislation and current control of the public moneys. The making of a plan or design for a long period of future years, a period which will cover the incumbency of many successive councils, is an entirely different type of work, raises problems which involve different factors, and requires different qualifications. The board which has this work in charge should be free from the pressures of purely current problems. Consequently council, by virtue of the very nature of its functions and by virtue of its term of office, does not have the qualifications, the time, or the political status which would make it an appropriate body for this long-time planning work. That work needs to be intrusted to a board or body specially chosen for the purpose and given a place in the government specially appropriate to the nature of this planning work.[4]

> The regular administrative and legislative officials have most of their time and thought occupied with pressing current problems and are

---

[1]U.S. Department of Commerce, Advisory Committee on Zoning, *A Standard State Zoning Enabling Act under Which Municipalities May Adopt Zoning Regulations,* rev. ed. (Washington, D.C.: U.S. Government Printing Office, 1926).

[2]U.S. Department of Commerce, Advisory Committee on City Planning and Zoning, *A Standard City Planning Enabling Act* (Washington, D.C.: U.S. Government Printing Office, 1928).

[3]Ibid., footnote 8.

[4]Ibid., footnote 10.

most interested in these and in immediate results. The community needs, also, leadership in long-time thinking and planning, and this leadership, in the nature of things, can seldom be furnished by an official busy with the daily routine and subject to the daily purposes.[5]

Technical and clerical assistance is essential to success . . . . Every commission should be in position to obtain technical advice and assistance from a man or men responsible to it exclusively and independent of the regular administration.[6]

At that time (1928) such considerations appeared compelling—particularly if one mistrusted the local politicians elected to the governing board. But by the mid thirties, experience had already indicated that if planning was to be effective, it must be more closely integrated with the other agencies of the city government. In consequence, shortly before World War II, many administrators and professional planners strongly urged that the planning board (and the staff responsible to it) be replaced with a full-time planning department responsible directly to the city manager.

Nevertheless the planning board has continued up to the present as a major element in almost every planning organization, serving at least the following useful purposes:

1. It can devote considerably more time to planning studies and the development of plans than the busy governing body can spare from other duties, so its advice potentially has a much better basis than a decision that the governing board might otherwise make.

2. It is a means for involving leading citizens (who might be reluctant to run for political office) in efforts to solve local governmental problems.

3. It can give the professional planning staff (which is commonly composed of persons not native to the area) an educated response as to the probable desires and objectives of the community in specific situations.

4. It can help interpret the local plans to the community at large.

5. It can serve as a protection for the hired planner against pressures from particular citizens of the community.

6. It can sometimes furnish the excuse for a governing board to make a necessary but politically unpopular decision concerning the development of the community.

---

[5]Ibid., footnote 22.
[6]Ibid., footnote 26.

7. It can serve as a mechanism through which the activities of several local governmental units or agencies may be coordinated.

In considering its role, the planning board must always keep in mind that it is primarily an *advisory* body. It rarely makes final decisions; instead, it makes recommendations. To the extent that the governing board charged with the duty of making decisions has confidence in the soundness of the planning board's judgment, it will follow that board's recommendations; to the extent that it does not have such confidence, it will largely ignore the recommendations.

This means that the planning board must do its homework; it must delve into the underlying factors bearing on any decision with a thoroughness that will impress both the governing board and the community at large. When its recommendations are challenged, it must be prepared to support them with facts. It must not accept any studies or plans prepared by its professional staff without being sure that they have been carefully prepared and without understanding both what is stated and what is implied.

The board must be careful not to abdicate its responsibilities to its professional staff. A lay board may very easily accept as gospel the work of the experts assigned to assist it, and turn to them for the decisions it is charged with making. The board must always keep in mind that the planning expert rarely has roots in the community he or she serves. The planning expert knows what the principles of planning are, how the principles have been applied in other communities, and what the results have been. But the planning expert frequently does not have the intimate knowledge of the situation in a particular community that its residents have; he or she probably has only superficial understanding of many community attitudes and aspirations. It is in these areas that the planning board can assist the expert, as they together make the many selections among alternatives that go into the preparation of a plan or the drafting of regulations. The board members must remember that they and their children will probably be living in that community long after the professional planner has gone on to other jobs. They must respect and use the talents of the professional planner, but at the same time they must preserve their independence of judgment.

The succeeding sections address more specifically what powers and duties the planning board has and how it may best carry out its functions.

Organization

As soon as a new planning board has been appointed, it should assemble and organize for business. Normally, in the absence of a chair, it will meet on call of the mayor, the chair of the board of county commissioners, or a designated agent. As its first order of business, the board should elect a temporary presiding officer. It then should review the statute (enacted by the General Assembly) under which it was created and the ordinance or agreement (adopted by the local governing board) by which it was established. (See the sample ordinances and agreements in Appendixes A–F.) This will be its introduction to the job it has agreed to perform.

On the basis of this review, the board should adopt rules of procedure for itself (a simple set of rules is included in Appendix G). These may be designated temporary rules, pending more complete study by a committee of the board, or they may be adopted as permanent rules. Regardless, the rules can always be changed as necessary. The important point for the board to remember is that, as a public agency, it should comply with its own rules; if it desires to act in a manner different from that permitted by the rules, the rules should first be changed. The rules must, of course, be in compliance with the provisions of the statutes and the ordinances by which the board was created.

The rules of procedure should specify the officers to be elected or appointed and their duties. Ordinarily, a chair, a vice-chair, and a secretary will be sufficient. The rules may also provide for appointment of committees of the board, although at the outset a new board probably does better to operate as a whole. As a board acquires experience and its workload increases, it may provide for committees—on the general plan, zoning, subdivision regulation, or other subjects—to make preliminary reviews of matters coming before it.

Meeting dates will depend on the workload of the board. In a small town or a rural county, meetings are normally held once a month, but in larger units biweekly or even weekly meetings are not uncommon. In the early stages of a board's existence, while it is familiarizing itself with its duties, it may meet with greater frequency than it does later. Regularity of meetings is important, so that members may reserve particular nights as they schedule their personal activities. Some boards meet during the day, but it is generally found more convenient to meet in the early evening.

A regular meeting place is also desirable, particularly for a municipal planning board. A county or regional board, with a larger geographical jurisdiction, may desire to rotate its meetings from site to site, both to increase its familiarity with the total area under its jurisdiction and to make attendance at occasional meetings convenient for citizens in various areas.

As a public agency, advisory to the local legislative body, the planning board should expect to conduct its business in public, as required by the state's open meetings law (G.S. Ch. 143, Art. 33C). It should also keep adequate records of its proceedings, and these too must be open to the public.

Having adopted rules of procedure, the planning board should elect its chair and any other officers specified in the ordinance or the agreement creating it and in its own rules of procedure. It will then be formally ready for business.

Staff and Facilities

Most authorities agree that except in extraordinary circumstances, some form of staff support must be available to the planning board. Some of this may be clerical—personnel to set up meeting rooms, take minutes, and handle related duties. Of greater importance are professional or technical staff services. These may be furnished from a variety of sources, at the election of the governing board (see the discussion in Chapter 4). The planning board should ascertain what sources of assistance have been made available, and if it feels a need for additional services, it should not hesitate to call this need to the attention of the local governing board.

Subsequently it is up to the staff to determine, in conjunction with other local officials, what is needed in the way of working space, maps, aerial photographs, drafting materials, statistical materials, etc., for the board and its staff to do an effective job. The planning board will be concerned directly with a need for two types of facilities: (a) rooms in which to meet and to conduct public hearings and (b) materials for the direct use of its members.

What the board uses for meetings and hearings will, of course, depend upon what is available. The room should be large enough to accommodate comfortably the board and a reasonable number of spectators. Aerial photographs and maps of its jurisdiction should be available (perhaps on permanent display), to allow board members and others readily to identify the location of particular matters under discussion. There should be a bookcase and cabinets that can be locked, in which to store the board's library of publications, its records, its maps and similar materials, and subdivision plats and other data concerning particular proposals submitted to the board; having these materials readily available will greatly facilitate the work of the board. If public hearings are to be held in the room, it would be desirable to have facilities for using slide projectors and video-tapes, as well as tape recorders and/or camcorders.

The board should begin to acquire a library of planning materials and to encourage its members to make use of them. It will probably find numbers of such materials available from the American Planning Association and the Institute of Government. Having a local code of ordinances handy, together with copies of any studies and plans that have been made for the jurisdiction, is desirable.

Finally, each board member should be provided with some personal materials. These include a notebook in which to file copies of minutes of the board's meetings; a copy of the ordinance or the agreement that created the board and a copy of its rules of procedure; and up-to-date copies of any existing zoning ordinance, subdivision regulations, and other ordinances (such as sign regulations) that are relevant to the board's duties.

Orientation

As soon as professional staff assistance becomes available to the planning board, it should call upon the staff to provide it with general background knowledge as to the scope of the proposed planning program. Regular sessions for the board's own education are highly desirable; otherwise, it will tend to become totally immersed in routine administrative activities and lose sight of the larger picture.

The planning board that wishes to be imaginative and effective should seek funds in its budget for activities designed to keep its members up-to-date with what other planning boards are doing in the state and around the country. One such activity is attending (with reimbursement for expenses) occasional national conferences of the American Planning Association, the annual North Carolina Planning Conference, other state and regional meetings of the North Carolina Chapter of the American Planning Association, short conferences (normally one to three days long) on particular topics held at the Institute of Government and other state and local institutions, the annual meetings of the North Carolina League of Municipalities and the North Carolina Association of County Commissioners, etc.

Another way of keeping up is through periodicals of the American Planning Association, the Institute of Government, the League of Municipalities, the Association of County Commissioners, and others. The board should subscribe to some of these periodicals and circulate them among its members.

No one ever learns all there is to know about planning. The best planning boards make deliberate provisions for the continuing education of their members.

Powers and Duties

The powers and duties of a planning board are spelled out in the many enabling acts pertaining to particular types of regulatory activities and in local ordinances or agreements. The board should ask its attorney to make available (a) the provisions of any special act or acts of the General Assembly that apply to the board, (b) the ordinance or the agreement that created the board, and (c) any local ordinances related to planning (such as the zoning ordinance or subdivision regulations) that may assign the board particular responsibilities. The discussion below is based in part on statutorily prescribed activities and in part on common practices.

Studies

G.S. 160A-361 (cities), 153A-321 (counties), and 153A-395 (regional planning commissions) all mention in a general way the responsibility of a planning board to make studies of the area within its jurisdiction and surrounding areas. The regional planning commission act amplifies this somewhat: "Study and inventory regional goals, resources, and problems." Although these prescriptions offer little guidance concerning the types of studies that can be made, they also contain no limitations on the scope of such studies. This is a matter that the board is free to determine for itself. Because planning is conceived to be a rational process, the board is free to seek any information that may bear upon the plans, the ordinances, and the recommendations it is asked to produce.

The planning board rarely makes any studies itself. This work is normally done by the staff, whether formal or informal. The board's role is to see that studies are initiated and carried out, to check on their thoroughness, and to review the soundness of the judgment that goes into their conclusions.

Plans

Unlike a number of other states (notably California) that mandate adoption of plans, specify in detail their contents, and require that local ordinances and administrative actions be in accord with those plans, North Carolina does not. (Such provisions have posed difficulties for many local governments insofar as they offer new grounds for legal attacks by landowners and developers unwilling to comply with local regulations.)

G.S. 160A-361 (cities) and 153A-321 (counties) merely impose duties for the board to "determine objectives to be sought in the development of the study area" and "prepare and adopt plans for achieving those objectives." G.S. 153A-395 (regional planning commissions) is again somewhat more explicit: "Prepare and amend regional development plans, which may include recommendations for land use within the region, recommendations concerning the need for and general location of public works of regional concern, recommendations for economic development of the region, and any other relevant matters."

Although most planning boards do not themselves prepare plans, they commonly play more of a role in such preparation than they do in the making of studies. This is because almost every plan involves (a) the setting of developmental goals or objectives and (b) the making of choices among several alternative courses that might be followed in attaining those objectives. In some measure these decisions involve technical considerations, and the board should quite properly defer to the better informed professional planner concerning them. In a great many instances, however, the technical factors will indicate that two or three approaches are equally acceptable; in this event the planning board should play the dominant role in making a choice. At the least the board should insist that the professional planner keep it apprised of how the plans are developing, so that it will understand what decisions have been made and why.

The statutes do not require that the planning board formally *adopt* any plans that have been prepared. However, such adoption, preceded by whatever public notice, hearings, and publicity the board deems desirable, serves several useful functions:

1. It forces the professional planner and the planning board to complete plans and not leave them in a half-baked, partially considered condition with many loose ends dangling.

2. It provides an occasion for the planning board to review and adjust the many minor decisions the board and the professional planner have made in putting the plan together, identifying inconsistencies and resolving them in advance of difficulties that they may otherwise create.

3. It should lead to greater familiarity with the details of the plan, so that the planning board will be more inclined to remember and apply the plan when making recommendations concerning proposed zoning amendments, subdivision plat approvals, and so forth.

4. It offers an occasion on which the public and the governing board can be informed as to the detailed contents of the plan and brought into the decision-making process before the plan is finally adopted.

5. It results in publishable documents that can be distributed to interested parties as concrete evidence of the local government's intentions concerning development.

Even though adopting plans formally is desirable, one caution should be kept in mind. There is a tendency, following such adoption, for a board to feel that its plan-making function is at an end. Nothing could be further from the truth. All plans must be reconsidered and revised from time to time in light of developments that have taken place since they were originally adopted. The validity of assumptions that were made originally must be questioned in light of further information that has become available. Experience may indicate that some decisions embodied in the plan were unwise. For these and other reasons, the board should set up a regular schedule for reviewing, revising if necessary, and readopting all of the plans that it has made.

Having prepared and adopted plans, the planning board should *use* them. Whenever it makes a proposal to the governing board, it should note how the proposal ties in with objectives stated in the plan; if the proposal conflicts with such objectives, consideration should be given to modifying the plan. Whenever it makes a recommendation to the governing board concerning adoption or rejection of a proposed zoning amendment, that recommendation should begin with the statement, "This amendment would [would not] be in accordance with our development plan." If the amendment is regarded as a desirable one, but conflicts with provisions of the plan, consideration should be given to whether or not the plan itself should be amended. The same is true of subdivision plat approvals.

If the planning board itself pays no attention to the plan as it performs its other duties, it can hardly expect the governing board, administrative officials, or the public to do so. As the plan's provisions come into contact with the real world, fuzzy and ill-considered provisions will be highlighted and can be deleted or improved.

Implementation of Plans

Although the planning board's plan-making function is one of its major reasons for being, the bulk of its duties quickly tend to become those concerned with preparation, amendment, and administration of various legal and other devices for carrying out the plans. Legal provisions concerning such duties are scattered throughout the General Statutes, but they tend to be concentrated in G.S. Chapter 160A, Article 19, for cities and G.S. Chapter 153A, Article 18, for counties.

Zoning

The zoning enabling acts for cities (G.S. Ch. 160A, Art. 19, Part 3) and counties (G.S. Ch. 153A, Art. 18, Part 3) assign slightly different responsibilities to the planning agency (planning board). G.S. 160A-387 provides as follows:

> In order to exercise the powers conferred by this Part, a city council shall create or designate a planning agency under the provisions of this Article or of a special act of the General Assembly. The planning agency shall prepare a proposed zoning ordinance, including both the full text of such ordinance and maps showing proposed district boundaries. The planning agency may hold public hearings in the course of preparing the ordinance. Upon completion, the planning agency shall certify the ordinance to the city council. The city council shall not hold its required public hearing or take action until it has received a certified ordinance from the planning agency. Following its required public hearing, the city council may refer the ordinance back to the planning agency for any further recommendations that the agency may wish to make prior to final action by the city council in adopting, modifying and adopting, or rejecting the ordinance.

G.S. 153A-344 of the county zoning enabling act contains essentially identical provisions to those above, but it continues thus:

> Zoning regulations and restrictions and zone boundaries may from time to time be amended, supplemented, changed, modified, or repealed. Whenever territory is added to an existing designated zoning

area, it shall be treated as an amendment to the zoning ordinance for that area. Before an amendment may be adopted, it must be referred to the planning agency for the agency's recommendation. The agency shall be given at least 30 days in which to make a recommendation. The board of commissioners is not bound by the recommendation, if any, of the planning agency.

Both the city (G.S. 160A-388) and the county (G.S. 153A-345) enabling acts also contain provisions allowing the governing board to "designate a planning agency to perform any or all of the duties of a board of adjustment in addition to its other duties." The board of adjustment normally has duties of hearing appeals from the zoning enforcement officer's decisions, making interpretations of the ordinance and its application to particular situations, granting variances in specified types of hardship situations, and issuing or denying special exceptions, special-use permits, or conditional-use permits, as the local ordinance mandates.

The planning board will probably wish from time to time to make studies aimed at the improvement of the zoning ordinance and to undertake a complete revision at specified intervals in light of changes that have taken place. It may initiate amendments at any time; frequently this will occur in response to situations that highlight deficiencies. In addition, property owners and others in its jurisdiction may request changes in zoning district boundaries, transfer of areas from one district to another, or changes in the text of the ordinance. As noted earlier, the county zoning enabling act mandates that these proposals be referred to the board for its recommendations. Most municipal zoning ordinances contain similar provisions.

In exercising all of these functions, the planning board will find that the best standard against which to test the ordinance or any proposed amendments is its previously adopted plan. Without such a standard to which it can turn, the board is apt to find itself caught up in the throes of a popularity contest between advocates and opponents of the proposal.

The nature, the contents, and the objectives of the zoning ordinance and the procedures thereunder are described at length in three Institute of Government publications: *An Introduction to Municipal Zoning; Legal Responsibilities of the Local Zoning Administrator in North Carolina;* and *The Zoning Board of Adjustment in North Carolina.*

Subdivision Regulations

Neither the municipal (G.S. Ch. 160A, Art. 19, Part 2) nor the county (G.S. Ch. 153A, Art. 18, Part 2) enabling acts for subdivision regulation assign responsibility to a planning agency for preparing such regulations or for making recommendations concerning them to the governing board. Nevertheless it is common for the planning board to take the initiative in recommending that such regulations be adopted and in preparing suggested regulations for consideration by the governing board. Proposed amendments to the regulations are commonly also referred to the planning board for its recommendations. Many ordinances and agreements creating planning boards contain specific directions that the board perform these functions.

Both enabling acts contain provisions (municipal, G.S. 160A-373; county, G.S. 153A-332) allowing subdivision regulations to specify that *final* plat approval is to be given by (a) the governing board, (b) the governing board on recommendation of a planning agency, or (c) a planning agency. Each of these routes has been followed by some local governments in the state. The enabling acts are silent, however, on the matter of approval of *preliminary* plats, which is actually the more important decision. This approval is required before physical changes (such as construction of streets and installation of various utilities lines) can be made on the land and before legal steps (such as designation of individual lots and dedication or reservation of land for parks and playgrounds) can be agreed upon. Almost always this approval is the responsibility of the planning board—not as a statutory requirement, but by authority of ordinance provisions.

Enforcement of subdivision regulations offers the planning board one of its major opportunities to influence new physical development in the community. To do this most effectively, it should have previously prepared plans to guide its requirements for major thoroughfares, open spaces, school sites, etc. By consulting these plans, it can determine what to require of each developer in turn and thus ensure that the piecemeal development of the community will ultimately produce a coherent whole.

There are many publications available that will assist the planning board in exercising this function, from such agencies as the Institute of Government, the American Planning Association, and the Urban Land Institute. In addition, the board should seek the advice of full-time city or county governmental personnel with expertise concerning particular types of improvements—the engineer, personnel of the street or utilities departments, etc.

Other Regulations

Chapter 3 notes other responsibilities that may be assigned to the planning board. Among these are serving as a historic district commission or a historic properties commission and assisting an economic development commission in its functions. The enabling legislation for urban redevelopment assigns the planning board responsibilities for designating redevelopment areas, certifying that redevelopment plans are in conformity with its comprehensive plan for the area, and making recommendations concerning the redevelopment plans for particular areas.

Apart from these assignments, the board should take responsibility for identifying needs for other types of regulatory programs for community improvement. It may well take the initiative in preparing and recommending adoption of such regulations as a sign ordinance, a street tree ordinance, a street-naming and house-numbering ordinance, a minimum-housing-standards ordinance, a junked-car ordinance, a weed-control ordinance, a greenway ordinance, or even a noise ordinance.

Recommendations as to Public Facilities

Plans for the provision of public facilities constitute a major segment of all community plans. *Public facilities* means streets, water and sewerage systems, parks and playgrounds, schools, libraries, museums, auditoriums, city and county offices, garages and storage yards, parking lots, courthouses, hospitals, and so forth. The local government is concerned that such facilities be properly located, be adequate in size and design to meet existing and anticipated needs, be provided at such times as best fit a program meeting the community's total needs, be provided as cheaply and efficiently as possible, and be protected against discordant neighboring development (whether public or private) that would prematurely destroy their utility.

In theory the mere adoption and publication of plans for the area should ensure that departments responsible for acquisition or construction of public facilities will fit them into the plans and meet the foregoing concerns. In practice all too many local governmental departments operate in relative isolation, and unless there is a definite procedure to ensure that individual projects will fit into an overall plan, they will not. For this reason many ordinances creating planning boards contain provisions that all proposals for public projects be referred to the planning board for its recommendations before other actions are taken. The planning board is expected to ensure that consideration is given to larger aspects that might be overlooked by departmental officials.

The planning board should show some restraint in the exercise of this function and not concern itself with such matters as details of construction, on which it is not really qualified to pass judgment. The following statements from the annotations of *A Standard City Planning Enabling Act* elaborate on this point:

> [A] planning commission should view all these phases of a city's development in a broad and comprehensive fashion and should not concern itself with detailed administrative duties which rightfully belong to other branches of the government. It should not, for example, be required to pass on details of street elevations or details of construction which the city engineer is best equipped to determine.
>
> The planning commission's function in such matters is to make a general design as to location, which it is especially competent to do in view of its knowledge of the city and the probable trend of the city's future growth. The regular city department or board concerned should ordinarily decide the advantages and disadvantages of specific lots within a given range or area. It may consult the planning commission during the negotiations and should, in any event, submit its final decision as to location to the commission. For instance, the commission should prepare the major thoroughfare plan showing the future new streets and extensions and their general conformity to existing conditions and topographic features. When the time comes for building the streets, then the selection of a more specific location may depend on a considerable number of factors, such as cost of construction, or of land, or engineering details of one type or another; and this part of the work is best worked out by the city engineer, whose decision is subject to general review by the planning commission, and similarly as to parks and all other classes of public works and improvements and utilities.[7]

In other words, the planning board should concern itself only with the details of location, size, access, etc., that affect other elements of its plan. It should not put itself in a position that officials may regard as meddling for the sake of meddling.

In general, too, the planning board and its staff should keep a close eye out for new proposals for improvements. This will enable it to offer suggestions to the departments concerned at a very early stage, before they have invested so much in planning a project that they are reluctant to make any changes.

---

[7]U.S. Department of Commerce, Advisory Committee on City Planning and Zoning, *A Standard City Planning Enabling Act,* footnote 31.

Capital Improvements Program

A more organized procedure for ensuring that public projects fit into the plan is the preparation of a capital improvements program. Not every unit has such a program, and not every planning board in a unit with such a program participates in its making. However, capital improvements programming has many advantages, and the board should be aware of its nature. Essentially the capital improvements program is a detailed schedule of the capital improvements that the unit expects to undertake within a given period (six years is the most popular).

The process of capital improvements programming works like this: Each year all department heads submit a list (with justifications and estimated costs) of the projects they feel their departments should undertake in the near future. Suggestions for improvements are also received from other sources. These are then considered together, and tentative priorities are assigned. At the same time the unit's financial picture over the next six or seven years is analyzed to determine how much capacity it will have to make expenditures. On the basis of the list of needs and the estimate of financial capacity, a year-by-year program is then put together, listing the projects that will be undertaken and the way in which they will be financed. The first year's projects go into the capital improvements budget for that year, and there is a five-year program of future projects on which detailed planning, financial arrangements, etc., can begin. Each year the process is repeated, so that there is always a program extending some distance into the future.

The planning board's role in this process (in jurisdictions in which it plays a part) is in considering and making recommendations concerning the priorities of the various projects and their relationship to other elements in its plan. Usually the local finance officer makes the financial analyses, and the manager and the governing board make the ultimate decisions as to what is included in the program and what is excluded.

Municipal Policies

Municipal policies governing such matters as utilities extensions, street improvements, and local assessments may have a major impact on the development of the unit. Although it has no direct responsibility with respect to such policies, the planning board should be aware of their importance and should be prepared to make recommendations now and then as to how particular policies might be improved or used more effectively.

Annexations

As cities grow, municipal boundaries must be extended from time to time to prevent unfortunate lapses in governmental services. North Carolina municipalities are uniquely fortunate in their ability to annex adjacent areas on the basis of statutory standards, without having to resort to the General Assembly, the courts, or the electorate. Under legislation originally enacted in 1959, a municipality can annex by the mere passage of an ordinance. But the areas must meet prescribed standards, and the municipality must have definite plans to furnish services to newly annexed areas at the same levels provided in other areas of the city. If the municipality fails to provide the services within a year, the annexation may be revoked by the courts.

The planning board has no direct responsibility under the annexation statutes. However, it is normally much concerned with all governmental measures relating to growth, and it should be prepared to study on occasion the desirability of annexing particular areas and to make recommendations to the governing body concerning such action. Not uncommonly, the planning board or its staff may be asked to make the studies necessary to determine which areas meet the statutory standards.

Extraterritorial Jurisdiction

Under G.S. 160A-360, procedures are set forth under which North Carolina cities may extend their planning jurisdiction over areas reaching as far as three miles beyond their city limits. Almost every planning board or its staff will sometimes be called upon to review the current limits and make recommendations as to whether they should be reduced or extended. Normally the staff will have major responsibility for designating proposed boundaries and identifying areas within which it is particularly important that the city exercise regulatory powers. However, the planning board may be requested to make recommendations concerning modifications. When a municipality asserts such jurisdiction, G.S. 160A-362 requires that residents of the extraterritorial area be added to the city's planning board and board of adjustment; normally these appointments are made by the board of county commissioners.

Reports

Formerly North Carolina's enabling legislation for planning required that every planning board make an annual report to the governing board giving information regarding the condition of the unit and any plans or proposals for its development. This is no longer true, but G.S. 153A-397 still requires annual reports from regional planning commissions.

Although reporting can be looked upon as a chore, it should be regarded as an opportunity to review the year's activities (for the planning board's own benefit as well as the governing board's) and to better inform the governing board and citizens at large of the work and the objectives of the planning board and ways in which the work might be made more fruitful. The board should not dismiss this opportunity lightly.

American Planning Association

The planning board should give serious consideration to joining the American Planning Association. This organization currently has two offices: one at 1776 Massachusetts Avenue, N. W., Washington, DC 20036; the other at 1313 East 60th Street, Chicago, IL 60637 (the address through which its many publications are available). The association holds a national planning conference each year and sponsors a wide variety of educational programs. It has a North Carolina chapter, which serves as a cosponsor of the annual North Carolina Planning Conference and holds several other conferences on specialized subjects each year.

The association's members include both professional planners and local board members. It is probably the single most important source of information concerning planning problems and solutions throughout the country, and many of its publications are the standard texts with regard to such matters. It is a resource that should be used by every planning board.

6

The Planning Staff

Although professional planners antedated the planning board as an element in American planning, the planning profession as a source of staff assistance is a relatively new one. As noted in Chapter 1, many early American cities were planned in some degree, at least with respect to their initial physical layout. This planning was commonly done by engineers or land surveyors, sometimes against a background of planning principles derived from European cities and sometimes in a highly mechanical gridiron fashion. These early planners rarely became a part of the government of the towns they had planned, and there was no continuing planning activity of the types described earlier in this book.

In the latter half of the nineteenth century, there appeared what might with greater accuracy be described as the beginnings of today's planning profession. This took the form of landscape architects (notably, at the outset, Frederick Law Olmsted, designer of New York City's Central Park and many others), architects (most significantly Daniel H. Burnham, who won worldwide acclaim for his 1909 Plan of Chicago), and civil engineers, who made careers as consultants in the design of cities or particular elements thereof.

Beginning in the 1920s, it became evident that something more was needed than the occasional services of consultants (unkindly characterized by one observer as "the peripatetic high priests of planning"), and there began a gradual development of resident, full-time planning staffs in the larger cities of the country. This movement generated a rapidly growing market for trained planners, which in turn led to a proliferation of university courses, departments, and schools designed to meet this demand. By the 1930s there was no doubt that a full-scale planning profession had emerged, and it has expanded exponentially in the years since that time. As early as 1917 a professional association had been formed, which became the American Institute of Planners and then today's American Institute of Certified Planners. A few states have now introduced licensing procedures for planners similar to those for practitioners in law, medicine, engineering, architecture, and other learned professions.

North Carolina trailed the rest of the country in this development. The work of consultants represented the sum of planning services available to the state's cities until after World War II. A few professional staffs were established in the larger cities in the immediate postwar period. Since then a succession of federal programs (most notably, urban renewal and community development) providing financial assistance for planning has led to a profusion of city and county planning departments throughout the state, largely staffed with professionals.

The University of North Carolina at Chapel Hill established in 1946 a graduate Department of City and Regional Planning for the education of professional planners, which very rapidly took its place among the foremost schools, departments, and programs of this type in the country. In the succeeding years East Carolina University, Appalachian State University, the University of North Carolina at Greensboro, the University of North Carolina at Charlotte, and Pembroke State University established undergraduate programs for such training.

Even so, the current demand for trained planners far exceeds the supply. A compromise staffing arrangement has become necessary in many of the state's smaller towns and counties—what might be called a quasi-resident staff. This consists of services made available on a contract basis through regional offices of the state's Department of Natural Resources and Community Development or through the eighteen regional councils of governments that blanket the state. In effect this arrangement permits the shared use of professional personnel by many small towns and counties that cannot afford (and perhaps do not need) the full-time services of a planning staff. Even where there are full-time staffs, consultant planners continue to play a role, performing specific services that the full-time staffs lack the time or the specialized background to furnish effectively.

Organizational Relationships

As planning organizations have evolved, two patterns have been predominant. For easy reference, they are here called the independent planning board and the planning department.

Under the independent-planning-board pattern, the planning staff is hired by and directly responsible to the planning board. This is the traditional pattern urged in annotations to the *Standard City Planning Enabling Act,* quoted in Chapter 5: "Every commission should be in position to obtain technical advice and assistance from a man or men responsible to it exclusively and independent of the regular administration."[1] With this arrangement the planning staff may on occasion make studies and recommendations for the city or county manager or the governing board, but most of its advice is channeled through the planning board. This organizational pattern is especially applicable to joint planning boards and regional planning commissions, which are created to serve more than one local government. Serving many masters would obviously be difficult for the planning staff, so for simplicity it is made responsible to only one— the planning board. (However, even a joint or regional staff is sometimes made responsible primarily to a particular governing board or local administrator, especially when that unit agrees to pay a proportionally greater share of its budget.)

The second pattern, the planning department, is one in which the planning staff is hired by and directly responsible to the city or county manager (the administrative head of the city or county government). Under this arrangement the planning staff advises and assists the planning board as that board performs its statutory and ordinance duties (and in return the planning board advises the staff as it makes its studies and plans), but the staff's primary relationship is with the manager. On occasion the planning staff may be asked to advise the governing board directly, but its advice is usually channeled through the manager. This pattern is found in most of North Carolina's cities and counties that have full-time planning staffs.

Where there is only a consultant or part-time staff available (through contract with the Department of Natural Resources and Community Development, a regional council of governments, or another source), the relationships may become somewhat blurred, and it may not always be clear whether the staff is primarily responsible to the planning board, the manager, or the governing board. These lines

---

[1] U.S. Department of Commerce, Advisory Committee on City Planning and Zoning, *A Standard City Planning Enabling Act* (Washington, D.C.: U.S. Government Printing Office, 1928), footnote 26.

should be carefully drawn, so that all concerned can avoid controversies and hurt feelings resulting from misunderstanding of their respective roles and responsibilities.

Regardless of formal arrangements, most present-day planners have no doubt that the most effective and fruitful planning takes place under circumstances in which the planning staff has a close and continuing relationship with the manager. Also it is obviously desirable that the staff work harmoniously with the planning board and the governing board.

Further, it is imperative that the planning staff develop friendly relationships with department heads of the unit; with the staffs of such quasi-independent agencies as the redevelopment commission, the housing authority, the school board, the board of health, the board of welfare, and the recreation commission; and with personnel of such state agencies as the Department of Transportation. All of these agencies will from time to time take actions vitally affecting the local plan and its effectuation, and a lack of cooperation among their staffs can only lead to chaos.

Powers and Duties

Unlike the planning board, the planning staff will find that only rarely are its powers and duties spelled out by statutes. One or more local ordinances may set forth its organization, powers, and duties. Usually, however, there will not even be such written prescriptions; instead it will take oral directions from the person or the agency (the manager, the governing board, or the planning board) to which it is primarily responsible. Normally, when statutes or ordinances prescribe studies to be made and plans to be adopted by the planning board, the staff will be called upon to do most of this work. Similarly, when such laws require the planning board to make certain recommendations to the governing board, the staff will assist in the preparation of the recommendations.

There is always a temptation for the planning staff, as a group of professionals working with lay people, to take a strong lead, to attempt to make important decisions on its own, or even on occasion to go over the heads of officials and take its case to the public. Such actions are highly improper. The planning staff, like the planning board, is *advisory* in its functions, and it cannot expect its advice always to be taken in a system of elective local government. If it cannot accept this role with reference to particular officials, then it should resign and move to a unit in which official views are more congenial to its own.

Internal Organization

Internal organization and administrative procedures of planning staffs tend to vary according to the size of the staff, the nature of the work to be done, the professional backgrounds represented among the personnel, and similar factors, so it is difficult to generalize. In most cases in which the number of personnel permits, a division is made between those concerned with preparation of long-range plans, those concerned with short-range studies, and those concerned with land-use regulations (such as subdivision regulations and zoning). Further divisions may be made on functional, geographical, or other lines.

Education, Training, and Qualifications

Any discussion of the education, training, and qualifications of the planning staff must be divided into two parts: that relating to the professional staff and that relating to the subprofessional staff.

Professional Staff

The basic education of professional planners, like that of doctors or lawyers, is furnished in colleges and universities before their entering employment. As previously noted, early American planners came from the so-called design professions—architecture, landscape architecture, and civil engineering. Their training in planning came largely through experience rather than from the classroom because there were no relevant courses offered. Then it became customary for university schools and departments in these professions to include courses related to planning within their curricula. This type of course offering has continued into the present.

Starting in the 1920s and 1930s, it became apparent that other specialties than the design professions should come into play when cities and regions were planned. Economists, lawyers, sociologists, geographers, political scientists, public administration specialists, traffic engineers, sanitary engineers, and many others were found to have something to contribute. As they entered the field, the same process seen earlier in the design professions was repeated: the schools and departments from which they came gradually began offering courses with a planning orientation. This too has continued into the present.

Finally, beginning with Harvard University and the Massachusetts Institute of Technology, a number of universities created full-fledged schools or departments for the training of professional planners. In most cases these offered master's degrees. More recently some universities have established doctoral programs (primarily for the training of faculty members), and some universities have begun offering bachelor's degrees or programs for planners (frequently as part of geography, political science, sociology, or related departments). As earlier noted, the University of North Carolina at Chapel Hill has a Department of City and Regional Planning that offers both master's and doctoral degrees, and numbers of other institutions in the state are offering bachelor's degrees.

The American Institute of Certified Planners (AICP), an institute within the American Planning Association, has a Planning Accreditation Board that accredits programs leading to planning degrees (based upon standards approved by AICP and the Association of Collegiate Schools of Planning). Table 1 presents its list of institutions with accredited programs for the period from September 1988 through August 1990.

In view of this history the educational backgrounds of professional planners today are extremely varied. However, there is an increasing tendency for the core staff in any planning agency to have recognized planning degrees.

As is the case with members of other professions, professional planners do not regard their education as coming to an end when they receive their degrees. Most of them expect (and should be encouraged) to attend one or more professional conferences each year as well as periodic short courses relating to new developments.

In general, the best preliminary test that a planning board or a governing board can make of the qualifications of a planner is to determine whether he or she has membership in the AICP. Planning vacancies are customarily advertised through publications of the American Planning Association (of which AICP is a part). The association also publishes periodic reports describing job titles, qualifications, and salaries in planning departments across the country. Publications of the North Carolina League of Municipalities and the North Carolina Association of County Commissioners offer in-state data on salaries.

Table 1
Institutions Accredited by the American Institute of Certified Planners
September 1988–August 1990

Alabama Agricultural & Mechanical University (BSUP, MURP)
University of British Columbia (MAP, MSP)
University of California, Berkeley (MCiP)
University of California, Los Angeles (MAUP)
California Polytechnic State University, San Luis Obispo (BSCiRP)
California State Polytechnic University, Pomona (BSURP, MURP)
University of Cincinnati (BUP, MCoP)
Clemson University (MCiRP)
University of Colorado, Denver (MURP)
Columbia University (MSUP)
Cornell University (MRP)
University of the District of Columbia (BSCoUP, MURP)
Eastern Washington University (BAURP, MURP)
University of Florida (MAURP)
Florida State University (MSP)
George Washington University (MURP)
Georgia Institute of Technology (MCiP)
University of Hawaii at Manoa (MURP)
Hunter College of the City University of New York (MUP)
University of Illinois at Chicago (MUPP)
University of Illinois at Urbana–Champaign (BAUP, MUP)
University of Iowa (MAURP, MSURP)
Iowa State University (BSCoRP, MCoRP)
University of Kansas (MUP)
Kansas State University (MRCoP)
University of Maryland at Baltimore (MCoP)
University of Massachusetts at Amherst (MURP)
Massachusetts Institute of Technology (MCiP)

Memphis State University (MCiRP)
University of Miami (MURP)
University of Michigan (MUP)
Michigan State University (BSUP, MUP)
University of Minnesota (MP)
Université de Montréal (BESSU, MU)
Morgan State University (MCiRP)
University of Nebraska–Lincoln (MCoRP)
University of New Mexico (MCoRP)
University of New Orleans (MURP)
New York University (MUP)
University of North Carolina (MRP)
Ohio State University (MCiRP)
University of Oregon (MUP)
University of Pennsylvania (MCiP)
University of Pittsburgh (MURP)
Portland State University (MUP)
Pratt Institute (MSCiRP)
University of Puerto Rico (MP)
University of Rhode Island (MCoP)
Rutgers University (MCiRP)
San Jose State University (MUP)
University of Southern California (MP)
State University of New York at Buffalo (MUP)
University of Tennessee (MSP)
University of Texas, Arlington (MCiRP)
University of Texas at Austin (MSCoRP)
Texas A & M University (MUP)
University of Virginia (BCiP, MP)
Virginia Commonwealth University (MURP)
Virginia Polytechnic Institute & State University (MURP)
University of Washington (MUP)
University of Wisconsin–Madison (MSURP)
University of Wisconsin–Milwaukee (MUP)

Legend

BAUP—Bachelor of Arts in Urban Planning; BAURP—Bachelor of Arts in Urban & Regional Planning; BCiP—Bachelor of City Planning; BESSU—Baccalauréat ès-sciences spécialisé en urbanisme; BSCiRP—Bachelor of Science in City & Regional Planning; BSCoRP—Bachelor of Science in Community & Regional Planning; BSCoUP—Bachelor of Science in Community & Urban Planning; BSUP—Bachelor of Science in Urban Planning; BSURP—Bachelor of Science in Urban & Regional Planning; BUP—Bachelor of Urban Planning; MAP—Master of Arts (Planning); MAUP—Master of Arts in Urban Planning; MAURP—Master of Arts in Urban & Regional Planning; MCiP—Master of City Planning; MCoP—Master of Community Planning; MCiRP—Master of City & Regional Planning; MCoRP—Master of Community & Regional Planning; MP—Master in/of Planning; MRCoP—Master of Regional & Community Planning; MRP—Master of Regional Planning; MSCiRP—Master of Science in City & Regional Planning; MSCoRP—Master of Science in Community & Regional Planning; MSP—Master of Science (Planning) or Master of Science in Planning; MSUP—Master of Science in Urban Planning; MSURP—Master of Science in Urban & Regional Planning; MU—Maîtrise en urbanisme; MUP—Master of Urban Planning; MUPP—Master of Urban Planning & Policy; MURP—Master in/of Urban & Regional Planning

Nonprofessional Staff

Every planning staff requires the services of people who do not have planning or other professional degrees—especially draftsmen, secretaries, and clerical personnel. These are normally hired through the local government's regular personnel procedures.

Regardless of their specific jobs, most such personnel will benefit from a general orientation concerning local planning, so that they can see how their particular jobs fit into a larger picture. Short courses in planning are frequently offered in-state through the Institute of Government, local assistance offices of the Department of Natural Resources and Community Development, some regional planning agencies, and such out-of-state institutions as Georgia Institute of Technology and Massachusetts Institute of Technology. Further, nonprofessional personnel are welcome at the periodic meetings of the North Carolina Chapter of the American Planning Association, the annual North Carolina Planning Conference, the meetings of the North Carolina Association of Zoning Officials, and gatherings of other organizations.

In addition to these opportunities for training, the International City Management Association offers correspondence courses in planning, and there are many publications that can be studied without supervision. The professional planner will usually be glad to guide nonprofessional staff members in a program of self-education.

Consultants

As already indicated, even when there are full-time professional planners at work in a local government, there may be some necessity to hire consultants to perform particular tasks. The need is obviously greater when there are no full-time planners available. Many units have no experience in contracting with such consultants.

Several years ago the American Institute of Certified Planners and the American Society of Consulting Planners promulgated the following statements for the guidance of units hiring consultant planners:[2]

---

[2]American Institute of Certified Planners and American Society of Consulting Planners, *Selecting a Professional Planning Consultant* (Washington, D.C.: American Institute of Certified Planners; Greenbelt, Md.: American Society of Consulting Planners, 1984), pp. 1–6. © 1984 by the American Institute of Certified Planners and the American Society of Consulting Planners. Reprinted by permission. A footnote in the original source has been omitted.

SECTION I

A Recommended Procedure for Selecting a Professional Planning Consultant

Organizations seeking professional planning services from consulting firms are sometimes perplexed as to what procedures should be followed in order to assure the selection of the most suitable and qualified firm. Proper procedures in the selection of a planning firm can also help avoid wasted motion in contract negotiations and execution.

A RECOMMENDED PROCEDURE. The following basic procedural steps are recommended as an ethical, businesslike, and systematic approach to the task of selecting a planning firm:

1. Define the nature of the assignment sufficiently to permit proper choice of consultants to be considered.
2. Consider the general qualifications of a number of firms which appear to be capable of meeting the requirements of the assignment. The size of the planning firm is not necessarily an indication of competence or suitability for the particular planning work or project being considered.
3. Choose for interviews firms (preferably not more than three) which are believed to be the best qualified.
4. Interview the selected firms separately, explaining fully the proposed assignment and the selection procedure to be followed. Carefully examine the qualifications of each firm by interviewing not more than one at a time, scheduling adequate time for each interview and spacing interviews to allow time for deliberation on each firm. Take into account especially the following criteria:
   - **Experience and Reputation.** It is essential that the client be fully satisfied that the firm has had experience that is relevant to the project. Direct experience in planning, in either a consulting or public planning agency capacity is a reliable source of know-how in the planning field, where success may depend upon the application of solutions successfully attempted elsewhere.
   - **Background of Personnel Available.** A professional planning education on the part of the specific personnel to be assigned is important, but this should not be the exclusive criterion used in selection. Credentials of the project manager and other key participants are also important.
   - **Workload.** Ethical firms do not undertake assignments that cannot be performed by their staffs in the time allotted. Frequently the client has no control over the precise time

when the assignment will start. Unless the work is to start immediately, the client's best assurance that the proper consultant staff will be available at the appointed time is the firm's reputation for promptness of performance and effectiveness of work. Reliance on the firm's professional reputation for service will ensure a high quality professional work product. Penalty clauses, performance bonds, bonuses for speed or other similar provisions are unnecessary in a professional services agreement.

- **Availability of Required Fields of Expertise.** Complex planning programs may require special expertise which a given firm may prefer to subcontract or perform in association with another. In such instances, the availability and reputation of subcontractors or associate team members should be as carefully considered as that of the principal contractor, as should the proven ability of the principal contractor to manage a multi-disciplinary team of independent firms.
- **Equal Employment Responsibility.** Reputable firms encourage and provide equal opportunities of employment for qualified women and members of all minority groups.

5. List the firms you have interviewed in order of desirability, based on capability for carrying out the assignment
6. Contact your first choice and agree upon a detailed program of work and mutually satisfactory fee. Unless the fee has been established in advance by the client, this should be the first time there is any discussion of fee.
7. In the event that it is found impossible to agree upon the work program, fee or other contract details, notify the firm in writing that negotiations are being discontinued. Then begin negotiation with the next firm on the list.

ADDITIONAL CONSIDERATIONS. Some pitfalls exist that can stall or frustrate negotiations. Once recognized, they can be readily avoided. Here are three examples:

- **Avoid Mass Interviews:** It is possible to interview too many consulting firms. The proper use of pre-interview selection techniques will enable the client to interview a few qualified consulting firms in depth and provide sufficient data for a sound selection decision. Every effort should be made to determine the experience of prior clients with consultants being considered.
- **Avoid Competitive Bidding:** Agencies are advised not to deprive themselves of competent professional assistance by insisting on a bid in competition with others. Competition is desirable; but it should be on the basis of professional competence and experience. Specific work assignments and fees should be discussed only after a consultant is selected. Even so, the lowest price does

not necessarily yield best results. If the agency has budgetary constraints for the assignment, it should make them known to all consultants.

- **Avoid Non-Written Agreements:** For the protection of both agency and firm, the agency should always execute a written agreement with a planning consulting firm. As a minimum, this agreement should specify the work to be done and the compensation therefor. The firm cannot be expected to do work outside of its contract with the client unless the contract fee is amended accordingly.

MUTUAL RESPONSIBILITY. The agency or organization has its responsibilities in the selection and hiring of a planning consulting firm as outlined here. Equally important to the agency, however, is the professional obligation of the planning consulting firm to perform its work competently, in a professional manner and with a sense of social responsibility. The American Institute of Certified Planners and the American Society of Consulting Planners govern the ethical conduct of their members through their respective codes of professional conduct.

SECTION II

Services and Fees of a Professional Planning Firm

Major types of planning services are outlined here, and consideration is given to the ordinary factors involved in computing a fee for services that will be fair to both the agency and to the planning consulting firm.

GENERAL CONSIDERATIONS. It is not possible to establish standard fee schedules to govern the charges of professional planning consulting firms. Variables may be based on the extent and breadth of a consultant's experience as well as on the variety, quality and character of his work. Fees are also based on the scale, complexity and importance of the work.

In general, fees are based on the scope and complexity of the work as measured by the time of professional personnel required to successfully complete it; the experience, education, training and reputation of the firm's personnel; and the kind of planning service which the firm is prepared to provide.

MAJOR TYPES OF SERVICES PERFORMED. The following list is intended to be representative of planning consultant services:

- **Reconnaissance Surveys and Work Program Development:** This may include working with state and local officials and agencies in surveying needs and opportunities relating to physical, social and economic development and structuring a work program outlining the kinds of planning activities that should be undertaken to deal with the issues identified.

- **Planning Agency Organization and Administration:** This may involve advising planning agencies in staffing, organizing and developing programs required to carry out a variety of planning and development related activities.

- **Preparation of Long- and Short-range Plans, Policies and Programs:** This would include analyzing development problems in depth, establishing objectives, shaping alternative policies and programs, and evaluating their impact as a basis for preparing plans.

- **Technical Assistance and Special Planning Studies:** Such work might involve the provision of advice on urgent development problems or it could pertain to special functional areas of concern (e.g., development impact, environmental concerns, feasibility studies, business area revitalization, housing, programming and budgeting aspects of developmental programs, and recommendations on development codes and ordinances).

- **Continuing Planning Advisory Services:** Technical assistance may also be provided by a consulting firm on a continuing basis as a staff supplement or substitute, where appropriate.

- **Project Planning:** This involves the preparation of site and subdivision plans for residential developments, new communities, shopping centers, college campuses, industrial parks, neighborhood renewal and other similar projects.

- **Provision of Assistance and Testimony in Court Cases:** Often consultants assist in preparing cases in zoning and planning-related development litigation and in providing expert testimony. The range of services which a firm is in a position to provide will depend upon the disciplines and experience encompassed by its personnel.

TYPES OF FINANCIAL ARRANGEMENTS. The following are common financial arrangements used for the provision of planning and related consulting services:

- **Lump Sum Fee:** This arrangement is advantageous due to its relative ease of budgeting. However, it can be a problem for the agency and the consultant, since it is difficult to anticipate unknown factors which could be involved. There should be a definite statement of time limits and a provision for the adjustment of the fee. It is, of course, necessary that the program and responsibilities of the consultant be specified in enough detail to preclude mutual misunderstanding.

- **Fixed Fee—Plus Actual Amount of Other Expenses:** Beyond a fixed fee, the firm is paid for costs incurred in connection with the work; travel, materials, printing and other out-of-pocket costs directly chargeable to the job. A limit of reimbursable costs may be set in the contract providing for this type of financial arrangement.
- **Per Diem Fees:** This method is especially advantageous for irregular or indefinite assignments. It requires explicit understanding of the respective charge rates for personnel and as to what constitutes a "day" and how travel time and expenses are to be allocated.
- **Time and Charges with Maximum Upset:** This method combines the advantages of a budget limit with the flexibility to meet uncertain needs or to conclude work earlier than anticipated with resultant savings to the client.

Other financial arrangements may be tailored to the situation and the mutually expressed concerns of the client and the consultant.

COST FACTORS. In calculating fees, a planning consultant must include, as a part of "overhead," the costs of operating a professional office. In addition, there is the time that must be spent in arranging for consulting work and attending professional meetings, as well as time for vacation and illness, none of which time can be charged to a specific client. Furthermore, every consultant must keep the nucleus of a competent staff and major equipment (such as computer systems) in readiness to serve at all times.

The AICP's *Code of Ethics and Professional Conduct* provides as follows with respect to responsibility to clients and employers:[3]

The Planner's Responsibility to Clients and Employers

B. A planner owes diligent, creative, independent and competent performance of work in pursuit of the client's or employer's interest. Such performance should be consistent with the planner's faithful service to the public interest.

1) A planner must exercise independent professional judgment on behalf of clients and employers.

2) A planner must accept the decisions of a client or employer concerning the objectives and nature of the professional services to be performed unless the course of action to be pursued involves conduct

---

[3]American Institute of Certified Planners, *Code of Ethics and Professional Conduct* (Washington, D.C.: American Institute of Certified Planners, 1981). Reprinted by permission.

which is illegal or inconsistent with the planner's primary obligation to the public interest.

3) A planner must not, without the consent of the client or employer, and only after full disclosure, accept or continue to perform work if there is an actual, apparent, or reasonably foreseeable conflict between the interests of the client or employer and the personal or financial interest of the planner or of another past or present client or employer of the planner.

4) A planner must not solicit prospective clients or employment through the use of false or misleading claims, harassment or duress.

5) A planner must not sell or offer to sell services by stating or implying an ability to influence decisions by improper means.

6) A planner must not use the power of any office to seek or obtain a special advantage that is not in the public interest nor any special advantage that is not a matter of public knowledge.

7) A planner must not accept or continue to perform work beyond the planner's professional competence or accept work which cannot be performed with the promptness required by the prospective client or employer, or which is required by the circumstances of the assignment.

8) A planner must not reveal information gained in a professional relationship which the client or employer has requested be held inviolate. Exceptions to this requirement of non-disclosure may be made only when (a) required by the process of law, or (b) required to prevent a clear violation of law, or (c) required to prevent a substantial injury to the public. Disclosure pursuant to (b) and (c) must not be made until after the planner has verified the facts and issues involved and, when practicable, has exhausted efforts to obtain reconsideration of the matter and has sought separate opinions on the issue from other qualified professionals employed by the client or employer.

7

Plan-Effectuation Agencies

The local government contemplating a planning program must think of creating and supporting not only a plan-*making* agency but also plan-*effectuation* agencies. The rationale for this is as follows:

1. The objective of a planning program is not the production of plans, but the production of some impact on development; plans are merely a means to achieve this end.
2. If plans are to have such an impact, they must be given a cutting edge in the form of (a) appropriations for public facilities and (b) regulations of private conduct.
3. Although the governing board and the plan-making agency may play a role in the expenditure of funds for public facilities and the administration of regulations, the scope of the work involved is such that they cannot handle it alone; this means that they must either assign additional functions to existing agencies or create new agencies to perform such functions.

Thus the plan-effectuation agencies must take their place alongside the governing board, the planning board, and the planning staff as essential components of the planning organization.

The local governmental agencies involved with the detailed planning, acquisition, construction, and operation of public facilities proposed by the plan may include at one time or another virtually every agency in the government. However, the nature of their activities in providing facilities pursuant to a plan is not basically different from the nature of their activities in providing facilities in the absence of a plan. For that reason they do not receive special coverage in these materials.

Other agencies (notably those involved with land-use regulation) must be created solely for the purpose of carrying out elements of the plan. Chief among these agencies are those that administer subdivision regulations, the zoning ordinance, building and housing codes, urban renewal programs, and economic development programs. Their respective roles are outlined in the sections that follow.

Subdivision Regulations

With regard to most types of regulations, the roles of the planning board and the governing board are limited to advisory or legislative ones: preparing, adopting, and from time to time amending the regulations. In the special case of subdivision regulations, these two boards play an additional role in administering the regulations because they are normally responsible for approval of proposed subdivision plats.

The planning staff also becomes more directly involved in the day-to-day regulation of subdivisions than it does in most regulatory processes. In addition to advising the planning board and the governing board as they exercise their functions, the planning staff quite commonly is called upon to negotiate directly with the developer in the early stages of the subdivision-approval process.

G.S. 153A-332 of the county subdivision-regulation enabling act includes this mandate:

> The ordinance shall provide that the following agencies be given an opportunity to make recommendations concerning an individual subdivision plat before the plat is approved:
>
> (1) The district highway engineer as to proposed streets, highways, and drainage systems;
>
> (2) The county health director as to proposed water or sewerage systems;
>
> (3) Any other agency or official designated by the board of commissioners.

Even in the absence of such a mandate in the municipal enabling act (and in addition to the mandates of the county act), the governing board may well ask for recommendations from such officials as the city or county engineer, the public works director, the water and sewer superintendent, the street superintendent, the school superintendent, and the recreation director. A second function that usually involves many of the same officials consists of inspecting and approving the manner of construction of streets, utilities, and other improvements built as part of a subdivision.

Zoning

The basic function of the planning board, the governing board, and the planning staff in connection with the zoning ordinance is the legislative one of preparing, adopting, and amending the ordinance. However, all three may be called upon to perform limited administrative functions under the ordinance, notably in the granting of special- or conditional-use permits. They may, in the exercise of these functions, informally call upon other officials (such as the city attorney or the zoning enforcement officer) for recommendations.

Fundamental responsibility for administering the zoning ordinance rests on a zoning enforcement officer (sometimes called a zoning administrator). In most North Carolina cities, towns, and counties, a building inspector (or an inspection department) is given this responsibility. In some of the larger cities in other states, a separate department of zoning administration has been created. In some cases the zoning enforcement officer is a member of the planning department. A number of cities have created a community development department that includes the personnel and the functions of planning, community development (or urban renewal), building inspection, and zoning enforcement.

Regardless of the organizational pattern, there must be an agency or official charged with (a) issuing, denying, and occasionally revoking zoning permits; (b) making regulatory inspections; (c) issuing certificates of occupancy or certificates of compliance; (d) initiating legal actions for the enforcement of the ordinance; and (e) keeping records, as well as performing miscellaneous other duties involved in enforcement of the ordinance.

Next, the zoning enabling acts (municipal, G.S. Ch. 160A, Art. 19, Part 3; county, G.S. Ch. 153A, Art. 18, Part 3) provide for the appointment of a zoning board of adjustment, normally composed of unpaid citizens, to hear appeals from the decisions of the enforcement officer and to grant certain special forms of relief under the zoning ordinance. Its basic functions are (a) to decide, on appeal, the proper interpretation of the ordinance as applied to a particular situation; (b) to issue or deny special permits (variously styled as special exceptions, special-use permits, or conditional-use permits) in situations specified in the zoning ordinance; and (c) to issue or deny variances in cases in which it finds that because of special circumstances the literal application of the ordinance to particular property would result in the owner's being unable to make any reasonable use of the property or derive any reasonable income from it.

The membership of the board of adjustment is specified in the enabling acts, together with a general description of its powers and duties. Most zoning ordinances elaborate somewhat upon the duties of the board and place additional limitations on its operations.

For additional information concerning the zoning administrator and the board of adjustment, see the Institute of Government publications, *Legal Responsibilities of the Local Zoning Administrator in North Carolina,* second edition, 1987, and *The Zoning Board of Adjustment in North Carolina,* second edition, 1984.

An additional zoning agency, the historic district commission, is authorized by G.S. Chapter 160A, Part 3A. This commission has primary responsibility (subject to appeals to the board of adjustment) for enforcing restrictions on the appearance of buildings and other structures in designated historic districts. Normally it works in close association with the zoning administrator and the planning board.

Building Code Enforcement

North Carolina has been almost unique among the states in having a State Building Code, promulgated by a State Building Code Council under the provisions of G.S. Chapter 143, Article 9. Although local governments may adopt deviations from this code, they can do so only with specific approval of the State Building Code Council, which has a policy of approving only minor variations. In 1977 the General Assembly mandated that all municipalities (G.S. 160A-411) and counties (G.S. 153A-351) arrange for enforcement of this code by specified dates (all of which have now passed). It further mandated that all enforcement personnel be trained and certified under a new Code Officials Qualification Board; a comprehensive program has since been put into effect by that board.

The Code Officials Qualification Board has established minimum qualifications for building, electrical, plumbing, and mechanical (heating and air conditioning) inspectors. With appropriate statutory amendments it is expected soon to add fire prevention inspectors to this list.

In general, inspectors issue, deny, and revoke building permits; make inspections; issue orders to correct violations; issue or deny certificates of compliance; bring judicial actions against actual or threatened violations; and keep appropriate records. For a more comprehensive discussion of these duties, see the Institute's publication, *Legal Aspects of Building Code Enforcement in North Carolina,* second edition, 1987.

Because these duties affect so many properties subject to other regulations, the building inspector is usually a key enforcement officer for plan-based requirements. At a minimum he or she is the official most apt to come across violations of the zoning ordinance, and his or her actions should be closely coordinated with those of the zoning administrator if they are not the same person.

Urban Renewal and Community Development

Most of the agencies described so far are concerned with new development within a local government's jurisdiction. However, local governments also have major problems relating to existing built-up areas that either developed in a substandard manner before any effective controls or have deteriorated with the passage of time. For many years such problems were attacked as isolated nuisances, but federal assistance in the 1950s and since has made possible more coordinated programs known initially as urban redevelopment, then urban renewal, and more recently as community development. Whatever its name, this type of program is an organized and planned effort to identify and correct conditions detrimental to the area and its residents through the coordinated use of various legal and administrative devices—ideally involving cooperation of private people, the local government, the state government, and the federal government.

What are the conditions at which this effort is aimed? A quick listing might include the following:

1. Poor construction of buildings; unsafe structures; fire hazards.
2. Inadequate provision for sanitary needs—water, toilet facilities, bathing facilities, window screens, sewerage system, drainage system.
3. Accumulations of garbage and rubbish, creating fire and health hazards, rodent and insect problems, etc.
4. Overcrowding in dwelling units; inadequate space, ventilation, etc.
5. Overcrowding of buildings on land.
6. Incompatible mixtures of land uses.
7. Inadequate or unsafe streets.
8. Inadequate recreation facilities, schools, and other public facilities.

Dealing with such conditions may involve actions like these:

1. Improved enforcement of the housing code, building code, zoning ordinance, health regulations, fire safety regulations, etc., in a coordinated manner.
2. Provision of better public services, such as garbage collection, street cleaning, street lighting, police and fire protection, and health and welfare services, in deteriorating areas.
3. Provision of improved public facilities, such as street paving, curbs and gutters and other drainage systems, water and sewerage systems, schools, and playgrounds.
4. Rehabilitation of individual structures.
5. Condemnation of particular structures or conditions as nuisances.
6. Area clearance for resale to private developers for new development (urban redevelopment).
7. Provision of public housing.

From this listing of conditions at which urban renewal or community development programs are aimed and some of the tools that are used, it will be seen that almost every part of local government participates (whether it realizes the fact or not). For maximum effectiveness, however, there usually must be a central agency to plan and coordinate the total program. This may be a housing authority, a redevelopment commission, a community development department, a planning department, or some other entity (in some cities, the coordinating function has been placed in the hands of an assistant city manager with a relatively small staff and perhaps an advisory committee made up of representatives of each department of the government).

At this time it does not appear likely that there will be a resurgence of federally financed programs on the scale experienced in the past, but state governments are taking increased interest. In the meantime local governments may wish to experiment with small-scale programs of their own.

Economic Development

Unlike the federal and state governments, North Carolina's local governments have traditionally limited their role in economic development. Until recently, most local planners went no further than to assist the local chamber of commerce, the merchants' association, or a similar organization with studies of population trends, resources, and sites for proposed facilities.

Lately, however, local units have become much more active in economic development programs. This process began with their getting authority to provide funds for advertising and other efforts to attract new industry. It expanded with the enactment of G.S. Chapter 158, Articles 2 and 3, allowing the creation of economic development commissions or industrial development commissions (whose powers were largely to develop economic development programs and projects and assist private agencies in carrying these programs out). This was followed by enactment of G.S. Chapter 159C, allowing counties to create "industrial facilities and pollution control finan-cing authorities" that could finance industrial projects, including the acquisition of land and construction of buildings. Finally, G.S. 158-7.1 gave all cities and counties (other than Buncombe) wide-ranging authority to engage in planning, land acquisition, construction, and other activities for the purpose of attracting and subsidizing new industries.

With this mix of statutory authorizations, no "best" organizational pattern has emerged. However, as pressures continue to grow for more and more governmental support for local economies, governing boards can confidently expect to receive demands for innovative organizational arrangements, most of a public-private variety.

8

Developing a Local Planning Organization

The preceding chapters give the administrator and the governing board a feel for what is permissible and what is usual in the way of a planning organization. But how do they actually design such an organization?

A General Strategy

Many architects say that "form follows function" in the design of a building. By this they mean that the designer should not begin with an image of the outside of a building (its form) and try to fit the various uses (its functions) of the building into this box; rather he or she should begin by analyzing the requirements of each of the projected uses of the building and their relationships to one another and *then* fit an exterior to the resulting structure.

The same principle applies to organization. Some administrators start with an ideal organizational structure based upon a chart in a book or a set of interconnected boxes reflecting span-of-control principles, and then assign duties to each of the organizational elements. The suggestion here is that this procedure be reversed— that the administrator begin with an analysis of the duties to be performed and desirable relationships between these duties, and derive from this the most appropriate organizational structure to accomplish them.

The process might start very basically with the questions, What is the purpose of the proposed organization? What are the objectives to be sought by its creation? Then one could think of the kinds of work and related activities that must be done to achieve these purposes and objectives. Broad tasks should be broken down into more and more refined subtasks, and consideration should be given to the sequence in which each must be accomplished. Finally, when there is a clear understanding of what has to be done in order to achieve the established objectives, it will be possible to decide what types of personnel and equipment will be required to perform the work and how they should be organized (grouped, directed, and supported) to perform most effectively.

Full-Time Staff, Citizen Board, or Both?

A fundamental factor to keep in mind is that organizational questions involve more than structuring full-time departments and agencies. As may have been noted from the enabling legislation set forth in Chapter 2, planning organizations are almost unique in local government in the degree to which they involve boards made up of appointed citizen members—usually part-time and frequently uncompensated. The reasons for this are obscure. In part they may reflect the fact that some drafters of early planning legislation were self-serving: they apparently wished to participate in plan making without committing themselves full-time to their local governments, so they created this type of slot for themselves. Second, in those early days there were few planning professionals, so there were no trained personnel available to most towns wishing to plan their future; they had to rely on part-time advisers. Third, unpaid (or low-paid) board members were obviously more economical (if less effective) than full-time staff members. Fourth, boards of this type were regarded as a mechanism for involving more citizens in the decision making of their local governments (and even as a training ground for future governing board members). Fifth, such boards could occasionally be useful to the elected boards when they wished to avoid total blame for making unpopular, though necessary, decisions.

Apart from the reasons just outlined, it is undeniable that most local planning efforts are strengthened when a conscious and continuing effort is made to bring about citizen participation in fundamental decisions. Sometimes there is expertise in the population that should be tapped when difficult problems arise. Sometimes it is important that the government provide channels through which citizens' views can be expressed to those in authority. Sometimes local governments feel a need to awaken a lethargic population to serious anticipated problems. To the degree that such needs can be met by creating ad hoc or continuing channels of communication and participation, local government is strengthened.

The governing board considering establishment of one or more citizen boards should begin by deciding what objectives are sought by such action. Although the statutory prescriptions for membership on citizen boards occasionally are quite precise, North Carolina's local governments are generally free to structure such boards as they wish. It is obviously inappropriate to think that a small board composed of residents of a particular neighborhood can be representative of the citizens as a whole or that a board of lay people can be given responsibility for reviewing the quality of architecture in a project. If the governing board feels a need for a channel through which it can receive advice from a cross-section of the community, it may create a very large and representative group (this is frequently the approach when a goal-setting operation is contemplated). If it wishes a more permanent arrangement encouraging involvement, it may foster the creation of continuing neighborhood associations (recognizing that such associations may become channels through which future political leaders may rise). If it wishes to take advantage of the expertise of particular professionals in the community, it may establish boards composed of people with special knowledge and experience (e.g., the statutorily prescribed membership of a historic district commission or a historic properties commission). Or it may simply ask that local associations of such professionals agree to furnish advisory or consultative services as needed.

In other circumstances boards could be constituted from among particular interest groups in the community—environmentalists, people seeking to improve the climate for economic growth, history buffs, and the like; the possibilities are endless. Some thought should be given to exactly what kinds of input are desired and how that input is best secured. (Certainly the widely mandated public hearings are not a complete answer to such needs.)

In creating citizen boards, it is well to recognize that they may pose problems. Governing bodies may create a wide range of special-purpose boards concerned with particular facets of land-use regulation or planning: historic district commissions, historic properties commissions, appearance commissions, environmental advisory boards, and others. Their rationale for doing this is that they can appoint members to each board who have particular qualifications and interests, who will focus very directly upon those interests, and who can be held responsible for results obtained. This is an *effective* way to organize, from many standpoints. But it is not the most *economical* way to proceed because each such board requires a meeting place, equipment, and staff services—for example, preparation and issuance of notices, preparation of agendas, and writing of minutes—not to mention the possibility of its needing professional assistance in carrying out major functions. Also, the multiplicity of boards is likely to lead to uncoordinated actions and policies unless further organizational arrangements (such as an umbrella board) are made to keep this from occurring. Finally, it is apt to impose considerable delays and red tape on the citizen who must appear before several boards before getting the permissions he or she needs to proceed with a project and who sometimes is caught between two boards with conflicting objectives. The governing board must balance these conflicting considerations and come up with a structure that best meets the needs of its constituents.

Objectives

A second issue to be addressed is the objectives the governing body and the administrator might consider desirable when setting up a planning organization.

A Central Source of Information

A rather basic level of planning involves the establishment of a central source of information concerning the area for which the governing board and the administrators are responsible. This ensures that when decisions must be made, they can be based on reliable data; without such data it is impossible to visualize the likely impacts of alternative decisions. The data must be made available to all appropriate agencies, so that they will operate with a common understanding of the situation. A surprising number of local controversies, both inside and outside government, stem from an absence of such an understanding.

To achieve this objective, the governing board may create a specialized library or a computerized data bank. Doing so requires that the board decide what kinds of information are needed; arrange to gather, organize, and store that information so that it can be retrieved readily; and see to its updating as necessary. This may produce needs for (a) people capable of deciding what kinds of information will probably be called for and ascertaining sources of that information, (b) people capable of doing the legwork of data collection under supervision, (c) people capable of analyzing information that has been collected and putting it into useful and usable form, and (d) people capable of installing and operating a system for storing this information and retrieving it on call. Depending upon the mode of storage that is selected, there will be various equipment needs: computers; shelving, file cabinets, and index files; or both.

There will also be support needs, such as building space, office equipment, and secretarial, janitorial, and other services. Finally, there must be managerial personnel. (Such an analysis is appropriate whenever a new organizational entity is proposed.)

Coordination

A second objective of the governing board and the manager might be better coordination among the different departments and agencies of the unit. The head of every organization yearns for a way to keep informed of what the various elements of the organization are up to, to minimize duplication of effort, and to avoid (where possible) interdepartmental conflicts. Although some coordination flows from a common data source, a more active approach to eliminating interdepartmental conflicts and duplication of effort would be creation of an interdepartmental committee made up of the heads (or their representatives) of all affected departments. Such a group could be charged with broad and continuing responsibility for developing plans, regulations, and policies for the unit. Alternatively there could be several interdepartmental groups with differing memberships, created to deal with specific areas in which two or more departments have overlapping responsibility. Or a series of ad hoc groups could be named to deal with specific matters as they arise.

Another approach would be for the governing board or the manager to assume the coordinating responsibility, relying on separate departments solely for information, review, and recommendations. If this proves burdensome, such coordination might be made the responsibility of one or more full-time assistant managers or a full-time planning department charged with keeping informed of actions by various departments and agencies that might impinge upon the activities of other departments or centrally established objectives.

Although the desirability of coordinating activities of departments is generally recognized, many units fail to consider the problem, mentioned earlier in this chapter, of coordinating the activities of the various boards that may be part of a planning organization. It is not at all unusual for the planning board to be moving toward one objective while the board of adjustment is moving toward another, and the housing authority, the redevelopment commission, and the historic district commission toward still others. Perhaps this suggests (a) creating a super board composed of the chairs or other members of all such boards; (b) overlapping some memberships; (c) holding periodic joint meetings; (d) designating certain members of one board to attend another board's meetings for a given time in order to serve as an interpreter between the two; (e) sending minutes of each board to all other boards; or (f) devising some other means of communication among boards. Whatever the solution, this problem must be addressed.

Efficiency and Economy

A third objective of almost every governing body is to achieve efficiency and economy in the unit's operations. This objective obviously has a close relationship to coordination. Through a failure of coordination one department may establish a facility on a site where it interferes with another department's operations, or one agency may duplicate another agency's facilities—such as a school system's duplicating the playing fields, the gymnasiums, and the auditoriums of the recreation department—with neither making use of them around the clock. The traffic department may paint fresh traffic lanes on a street just before it is repaved by the street department, and the repaving may be followed by the water department's breaking through the pavement to install a water main. All of this is wasteful.

Sometimes with a central property-management system an administrator will find that property being released because it has become excess to the needs of one department can meet the needs of another. This type of economy can be achieved through better coordination of the types discussed previously.

Other types of efficiency and economy are worthy of consideration; with proper planning great savings can be realized. If the need for sites for public facilities can be recognized well in advance, they can be secured while land is cheap and available. Some types of facilities, such as streets, water and sewer lines, sidewalks, and small recreational sites, can be secured entirely without cost to the general public through enforcement of subdivision or other regulations. Sometimes expansion is not considered when a site is acquired or a facility is built, and costly land purchases or facility extensions become necessary later. For example, if street rights-of-way are not large enough to allow for later widening, or if water mains or sewer outfalls are undersized at the beginning, great additional expense may be imposed over time. Streets may be continually closed for widening or for installation of new utility lines, and the public may be greatly inconvenienced.

On the other hand, facilities may be overbuilt. They may be designed for needs that never arise—sometimes because of the governmental unit's own restrictions on development—and the excess costs may be wasteful.

All of these problems could be avoided through intelligent foresight. Finally, there are some patterns of development that are much cheaper to serve than others, and these can be achieved through astute regulation.

To avoid waste or to secure savings of these types, the unit must develop a clear vision of the future—where it is headed (or desires to go) and how it can get there with minimum costs. This means that it should establish a formal planning program, with responsibility centered in one particular agency located (in an organizational sense) immediately adjacent to the chief administrator or the governing board.

Responsiveness

Yet another objective of the planning organization might be responsiveness to needs of citizens. As cities and counties grow, governing boards have less and less immediate contact with their citizens, and full-time officials may be even more remote. As noted earlier, this has led to creation of neighborhood associations in some units, giving citizens formal channels through which to indicate their needs and desires to appropriate authorities. Other units have created "branch city halls" as contact points. A less expensive approach is designation of officials to concentrate their attention on particular neighborhoods, with or without offices there. Some units simply direct all departments to make an effort to notify residents of any actions affecting their neighborhoods. An informed citizenry is thought by many to be a basic requirement of democratic government; unfortunately, many local governments do little beyond legally required public hearings and occasional bond elections to achieve such an electorate.

Beyond this fundamental type of responsiveness, of course, the governing board and the manager desire that the organization be responsive to their direction. This requires establishment of clear channels for transmission of directives, so that every member of the government knows what policies have been set. If policy directives never reach lower-level personnel, the entire organization is in trouble.

There must also be open channels through which information can come to the board and the manager from lower levels of the government. Some managers of local governments wish to be the only channel through which information and recommendations can reach the governing board, and some department heads, the only channel through which information reaches the manager. In the end such restrictiveness usually proves counterproductive.

Comprehensiveness

Finally, as has already been stated in varying ways, the essence of planning is comprehensiveness. By this is meant recognition of the interrelatedness of matters for which plans are made. All units of the government must recognize that they are not operating in a vacuum, that they must take account of the impacts of their efforts on other units. Without organizational, managerial, and other measures to ensure this, the result is destined to be a form of chaos. A common information source, coordination, efficiency and economy, and responsiveness: all are aspects of this one objective.

Part 2

Intergovernmental Organization

9

Intergovernmental Relations in Planning

To understand fully the problems in devising an optimum organization for local governmental planning, it is necessary to look beyond the internal organization of a particular governmental unit and see how the various planning functions might be allocated among or coordinated across several governmental units. In the usual North Carolina situation this necessity is particularly significant with respect to relationships between a city and the county of which it is a part. It is becoming increasingly apparent, however, that some areas of the state are encountering problems that can be solved only through regional (multicounty) cooperation or by action of the state government.

Long experience in carrying on planning programs has indicated that it is neither theoretically nor practically feasible to plan for and regulate the development of a small area without regard to its surroundings. Early planning was limited to the center of the city; then it extended to the city limits; next, cities received extraterritorial powers to deal with areas on their fringes; soon counties became interested; later came metropolitan planning agencies, state planning agencies, multistate planning agencies, and even federal planning agencies. This evolution led to the organizational problems discussed in this chapter.

It might be well initially to separate the processes of plan making, regulation, and provision of public facilities. Although it is undoubtedly true that maximum coordination is achieved only when these functions are united, other considerations may produce an organizational structure in which one or more are separated from the others.

Current Legal Jurisdiction

The analysis begins with a brief review of the existing pattern of legal powers to engage in planning activities.

Plan Making

Under the statutes there is authority for creation of city planning boards (G.S. 160A-361), county planning boards (G.S. 153A-321), joint planning boards (G.S. Ch. 160A, Art. 20, Part 1), regional planning commissions (G.S. Ch. 153A, Art. 19), regional planning and economic development commissions (G.S. 153A-398; 158-14), and regional councils of governments (G.S. Ch. 160A, Art. 20, Part 2) to engage in the making of plans. All of these agencies may be provided staff assistance.

In addition, there is statutory authority for a city planning board, a county planning board, or a joint planning board to make the services of its staff available, under contract, to another planning board. A regional planning commission may furnish technical planning assistance, with or without a contract, to local governments in its region. The same is true of a regional council of governments. At the state level the Department of Natural Resources and Community Development is authorized to furnish such assistance to local governments and planning boards (G.S. 143-323(c)).

There are no statutory limits on the territorial scope of the plans prepared by these agencies. Although a planning board of a particular unit will, of course, be most concerned with development inside that unit, it will inevitably be interested also in the setting of the unit. A municipality's planning board could hardly restrict its studies and plans to the areas within the current municipal limits, for example, if 75 percent of the municipality's growth was taking place outside those limits. Similarly it would be silly to attempt to forecast population growth or economic development for a small town with no consideration of county, state, regional, and national trends. For these reasons it is rare indeed to find a study or a plan that does not take some account of surrounding development, although the level of detail in the studies of larger areas will be progressively less, being dictated by considerations of cost, relevance to local problems, etc.

The plans of smaller units routinely extend beyond their boundaries, but there is no legal compunction for any planning board to take into account the plans of other planning boards. Unfortunately it is not unusual to find situations in which one city's plans overlap geographically with those of other cities, counties, or a regional planning commission but the plans are not congruent. The result of such situations is essentially the same as unplanned chaos.

Regulation of Land Use

North Carolina cities (since 1972) and counties (since 1974) enjoy virtually identical land-use regulatory powers, including power to regulate subdivisions; zone; establish and regulate historic districts; regulate historic properties; enforce the State Building Code; establish and enforce minimum housing standards; acquire and preserve open space; and carry out community development programs (G.S. Ch.160A, Art. 19; Ch. 153A, Art. 18). They may also regulate floodways and flood plains (G.S. Ch. 143, Art. 21, Part 6) and structures and trees in the vicinity of airports (G.S. Ch. 63, Art 4). Further, they each have more general regulatory powers (G.S. Ch. 160A, Art. 8; Ch. 153A, Art. 6).

Basically, county regulatory jurisdiction extends to all areas not subject to municipal regulation, and with the consent of the municipal governing board, counties may enter municipalities' extraterritorial jurisdiction and even cross over city limits. The basic municipal jurisdiction is within the city limits. However, unless the county has adopted and is enforcing subdivision regulations and a zoning ordinance and is enforcing the State Building Code in the area outside municipal limits, a city may extend its land-use regulations over a mapped area not more than one mile beyond its limits. Cities over 10,000 population may extend them up to two miles, and cities over 25,000, up to three miles, in each case with the approval of the county commissioners (G.S. 160A-360).

In addition, G.S. Chapter 160A, Article 20, Part 1, gives extensive authority for any two or more local governments to contract for joint operation of a function or for one unit to furnish services to another. Other sections of the General Statutes grant similar authority with respect to particular functions.

Other types of local governmental units may also have regulatory functions. Local *boards of health* may enact a wide range of health regulations (it is not unusual for them to include mobile-home-park regulations, waste disposal regulations, swimming pool regulations, weed-control regulations, etc.). These apply throughout the district —be it a county or a multicounty area. The governing boards of *sanitary districts* have certain regulatory powers under G.S. 130A-55. Their jurisdiction extends only to the limits of the district. The *Coastal Resources Commission* has authority to regulate many aspects of development in the coastal area of the state, as defined by G.S. 113A-103.

In addition to the General Assembly, most state departments and agencies have regulatory powers. Usually these apply statewide, although they may affect only limited geographical areas because of the nature of their subject matter.

Provision of Public Facilities

Public facilities means water and sewerage systems, streets, schools, parks and playgrounds, and so forth. As has been discussed, public facilities may be provided by governmental units in a manner intended to *influence* the pattern of development, or they may be provided *as a result* of development.

Many different governmental agencies have authority to provide one or more types of public facilities in North Carolina. Among these are cities; counties; combinations of cities and/or counties; special districts, such as sanitary districts, small watershed districts, soil conservation districts, drainage districts, and rural fire protection districts; authorities, such as airport authorities and housing authorities; and many state agencies, including the Department of Transportation, the Department of Natural Resources and Community Development, the various institutions of higher learning, the mental and correction institutions, and so forth. The General Assembly has power both to authorize these units and agencies to provide such facilities, and to grant funds or fund-raising powers to pay for them.

In general, municipal facilities must be established within cities' corporate limits, but there is explicit statutory authority for them to locate many facilities, such as reservoirs and sewerage installations, beyond those limits. Counties' powers extend to all areas within their boundaries (including municipalities within the county).

Objectives of Intergovernmental Organization for Planning

As in the case of developing a local planning organization (described in Chapter 8), developing an intergovernmental planning organization should begin with a consideration of objectives to be sought in the overall scheme. These objectives are essentially the same as those involved in selection of a local organizational pattern, but they may vary in their relative importance when applied to intergovernmental arrangements.

Coordination

Coordination refers primarily to managerial and administrative considerations. To the extent that local governmental functions are divided among a number of more or less independent governmental units or agencies, each seeking different objectives, there may be real difficulties. For example, a school board may build a new school on the only feasible route for a proposed major thoroughfare, or at a location such that every child attending will have to cross a thoroughfare to reach the building. Or a school board may build a new school in a residential neighborhood just before the redevelopment commission clears out all residences as substandard and sells the land for redevelopment as an industrial tract. The Department of Transportation may pave a street just before the local utilities department digs it up to install new water lines.

Offices of different agencies dealing largely with the same clientele may be so widely scattered as to inconvenience the public and hamper necessary contacts between their employees. Or they may be so located as to interfere with the operations or the future expansion of one another.

Regulations issued by different agencies may differ so widely in their enforcement procedures as to confuse the citizens being regulated. The developer who operates in several cities and counties may have great difficulty in learning the appropriate administrative channels to follow under their different zoning ordinances and subdivision regulations. In some cases different governmental units will compete with one another for development by offering less restrictive zoning or subdivision provisions. Adjoining units may produce adverse impacts on each other through their regulations; a city might be attempting to preserve a high-class residential area on its borders through highly restrictive zoning, only to have the county zone an abutting area for industry.

Obviously coordination becomes *more* feasible as the number of units and agencies involved in a planning program decreases and *less* feasible as the number of units increases. A single government with complete jurisdiction to plan, regulate, and provide all public facilities for a specified area would represent the optimum organization for achieving coordination within that area. In the absence of such unification, a wide number of arrangements and procedures may be employed to improve coordination.

Comprehensiveness

Comprehensiveness has three aspects. First, it is similar to *coordination* as defined here insofar as it suggests that the planning objectives for a given area should take into account all of the objectives of the various agencies whose programs may have an effect upon development of that area. Second, a *comprehensive* planning program should include all of the elements necessary for any *successful* planning program: it should give attention to all the interrelated factors that may affect development of the area, and it should make use of all available means for carrying out the plans that have been prepared. Third, the term has a connotation of geographical completeness: the comprehensive planning program should cover all of the geographical area that should be treated as a unity because of economic, social, physical, or other relationships.

Presumably the factor of comprehensiveness would in most circumstances indicate that the governmental unit authorized to plan, regulate, and provide facilities should have a large geographical jurisdiction as well as adequate statutory authority to carry on a complete planning program. These factors may not always be coupled. In North Carolina, for example, the county has broader geographical jurisdiction than the municipality, but it may not have the same willingness to exercise the full range of its powers; other units may have the willingness, but not the statutory authority.

Responsiveness

Responsiveness refers to the control that may be exercised over the planning process by the citizens affected. To the extent that these citizens are unable, through electoral or other processes, to make their desires felt by the decision makers, there is a failure in responsiveness. An example of such a failure may be seen in the planning organization of one of the southern states. There the governor appoints a state planning commission, which has authority to create regional planning commissions and appoint their members; the regional planning commissions in turn have authority not only to make studies and plans but also to adopt and enforce subdivision regulations. The only way in which a citizen dissatisfied with the content of such subdivision regulations can make a protest is to vote for another governor (not a major form of relief because the governor cannot constitutionally succeed himself or herself) or to vote for a legislator who has pledged to amend the state law under which this organizational scheme was created.

The factor of responsiveness is important in all three aspects of planning: the making of plans, the regulation of development, and the provision of public facilities. It becomes particularly critical when officials of the agencies with authority to regulate or to make decisions concerning provision of public facilities are appointed rather than elected—for example, when these functions are fulfilled by state agency staff or by locally appointed boards empowered to expend federal grant funds with a minimum of control by local elected officials. It is also an important factor with respect to the exercise of extraterritorial powers by municipalities. A third situation in which it may become important is when the decision-making power is placed in the hands of a very large geographical unit in which the citizens immediately affected have relatively little voting power.

Again, it is not always easy to give a straightforward answer to issues of responsiveness. At first glance it appears that zoning outside municipal limits should be done by the county, whose governing board is elected by the people affected. However, the immediate need for zoning may be to protect the interests of citizens of the municipality who are receiving adverse economic, health, and safety impacts from unregulated growth on their doorstep and who will be called upon to finance expensive corrective measures when the unregulated areas are later annexed. If most of the county's voters are little affected by the problem and do not wish the county commissioners to adopt a zoning ordinance, should the municipality be barred from exercising some control?

Efficiency and Economy

Efficiency and economy have a close relationship to coordination. When some facilities are located without reference to others, there is a palpable waste. There are other aspects of efficiency and economy besides coordination, however. The supply of professional planners, as has been noted, is not large in relation to demand, and their services are consequently expensive. It makes sense to organize in such a way that maximum use is made of these professionals. Next, through consolidation of planning staffs, enforcement staffs, engineering staffs, etc., it is possible to provide specialized services; to schedule work more evenly; to reduce overall requirements for office space, equipment, and secretarial support; and to effect other economies. Sharing of public facilities can also lead to economies of scale and other kinds of savings. When local governments are fragmented, they frequently must duplicate public facilities wastefully. In general, this factor suggests the desirability of larger-scale planning units and the elimination, in one way or another, of unnecessary duplication.

Equity of Support

In a sense, equity of support is related to comprehensiveness. This factor has to do with placing the burden of financial support for services on those who benefit from them. Because the need for land-use regulations and public facilities may be greater in urbanizing areas than in rural areas, account should be taken in developing a planning organization of how best to place major responsibility for financing those services on the urbanizing areas. It may be that the relative tax valuations of property in the two types of areas will yield essential equity of this kind. Alternatively a special taxing district, special assessments for particular facilities, creation of jointly supported city-county planning organizations, or other measures may be necessary to improve the relationship between costs and benefits.

Conflicts among Objectives

A moment's reflection will indicate that efforts to achieve these objectives may well conflict with one another in some manner. Emphasis on comprehensiveness, for example, may reduce the degree of responsiveness or the degree of equity of support in the proposed organization. When there are conflicting interests, judgment must be exercised to find the best accommodation among them.

Varying Means for Achieving Objectives

Obviously there is no single solution to any organizational problem. Almost any of the objectives may be achieved with varying degrees of success, under varying arrangements. Table 2 illustrates this. It shows how the coordination of planning efforts might be achieved at three levels of intensity (consolidation, formal coordination, and informal coordination) by a municipality and the county of which it is a part. The reader will note that coordination may be achieved at the level of the two governing boards, at the level of the planning boards, or at the level of the planning staffs. Furthermore,

Table 2
Intergovernmental Coordination of Planning and Land-Use Regulation

Level of City-County Coordination	Level of Intensity		
	Consolidation (Single Unit)	Formal Coordination	Informal Coordination
Governing board	City-county government or county taking over function on request (G.S. 160A-360(d)) or under contract (G.S. Ch. 160A, Art. 20, Part 1)	Statutory or ordinance provisions requiring (a) approval, (b) joint action, or (c) recommendations from other board before taking certain actions	Periodic joint meetings, exchange of minutes, ad hoc consultation
Planning board (or similar group)	Joint planning board (G.S. Ch. 160A, Art. 20, Part 1) or regional planning commission (G.S. Ch. 153A, Art. 19) or regional planning & economic development commission (G.S. 153A-398) or regional council of governments (G.S. Ch. 160A, Art. 20, Part 2)	Joint planning board composed of two or more planning boards of individual units, which continue to function separately as well as together Statutory or ordinance provisions requiring (a) joint action or (b) recommendations from other board before taking certain actions	Periodic joint meetings, exchange of minutes, exchange of studies and plans, ad hoc consultation
Planning staff	Staff working for (a) consolidated government, (b) joint or regional planning board, (c) regional planning & economic development commission, or (d) regional council of governments, possibly under contract to individual units	One unit's staff furnishing technical assistance to other unit under contract (G.S. 160A-363; 153A-322; Ch. 160A, Art. 20, Part 1)	Periodic meetings; exchange of studies, plans, and other information; division of responsibility for studies and plans of mutual interest

there is no reason why it cannot be achieved at all three levels simultaneously—or why one level could not have coordination at one degree of intensity while another has coordination at another degree. When this approach is applied to the processes of adopting and enforcing regulations and of providing public facilities for particular areas, additional possibilities for improving coordination will suggest themselves.

Major Alternatives in Local Planning Organization

Against this background, here are some of the major alternatives available for organizing local planning efforts:

1. Creation of a regional planning agency, with authority to make regionwide studies and plans and to furnish planning assistance (staff support) to local units within the region.
2. Creation of a regional planning agency, with authority as in *(1)* but with additional authority to provide regionwide facilities (water and sewerage systems, major parks, airports, etc.). This would require legislation combining several current types of authority.
3. Creation of a unified city-county government.
4. Transfer of the planning function from municipalities to the county, with the latter exercising sole authority to make studies and plans and to adopt and enforce land-use regulations throughout the county.
5. Transfer of all municipal extraterritorial powers to the county, with the latter planning, regulating, and serving all unincorporated areas (but municipalities continuing to serve the areas within their limits).
6. Continuation of the usual existing situation, with municipalities exercising planning powers within their boundaries and over designated extraterritorial areas, and the county exercising such powers beyond those areas.
7. Extension of municipal extraterritorial jurisdiction to cover a larger proportion of areas undergoing urban-type development.
8. Creation of new special tax districts with planning powers over larger areas than existing municipalities.
9. Creation of a joint city-county planning board—
   (a) as the only planning board for each of these units,

   (b) composed of the full membership of the city planning
       board and the county planning board, which continue to
       exist as such, or
   (c) composed of selected representatives of the city planning
       board and the county planning board, which continue to
       exist as such.
10. Creation of a joint planning staff for the city and the county.
11. Creation of joint city-county agencies (such as a joint inspec-
    tion department) for administering and enforcing planning
    regulations.
12. Creation of joint city-county agencies for providing particular
    public facilities, such as parks and libraries.
13. Transfer of responsibility for certain types of public facilities
    from the city to the county.
14. Use of various formal and informal measures to improve coor-
    dination between existing city and county agencies.

In making a selection of organizational solutions from among
such alternatives as these, local officials will wish to keep in mind the
objectives that have been stated and to consider how they apply to
each solution. In addition, the following somewhat more specific
considerations may be found helpful:

1. It is desirable that both plan making and measures to carry out
   those plans be under the control of the same governmental
   units.
2. It is desirable that regulatory powers be coupled with power to
   construct major public facilities that influence patterns of
   development—particularly major thoroughfares, water and
   sewerage systems, parks, and schools.
3. Any governmental unit exercising planning powers should
   have adequate geographical jurisdiction to cover the areas in
   which problems are arising or are expected to arise.
4. Because many counties have taken little responsibility for provision of public facilities other than schools, their primary
   interest in planning may lie, not in the efficient provision of
   public services and facilities, but in encouraging development
   of a sound living environment for their citizens and indirectly
   a strong tax base. The city is more apt to have both objectives
   in mind. This may produce differences that are reflected in
   basic differences in their plans.
5. Historically cities have had more interest in planning than
   counties, and urban citizens, living closer together, have been

more willing to accept restrictions on their conduct than rural residents have been. This means that cities are more apt to see a need for regulations and to be more vigorous in their enforcement than counties.

6. Cities are normally more tightly organized than counties, from an administrative standpoint; they have experienced officials and agencies in many fields associated with planning, whereas counties may have none. This means that cities may be reluctant to relinquish their planning powers to counties because of fear that required controls over development will be loosened.

7. Counties do not usually have uniform development (in an urban sense). Instead, the growth taking place, and the consequent willingness (or demand) of citizens to be regulated, may be patchy outside municipalities.

8. In situations in which cities exercise extraterritorial controls, there is less responsiveness to the wishes of the people subject to these controls.

9. In situations in which abutting areas are regulated by two separate governing boards, it is important that procedures and the general plan of regulations be similar.

Appendixes

The ordinances and the agreements set forth in these appendixes are offered not as legally mandated documents, but as sources of ideas for drafters of local instruments. Local circumstances and desires may well lead to extensive modifications of the phraseology and the substantive content. Statutory references are intended as guides to the General Statutes provisions that authorize the instrument in question or lead to inclusion of specific provisions. Italicized material in brackets [ ] represents optional provisions. Commentary is footnoted.

Municipal Planning Organization Ordinance

AN ORDINANCE TO ESTABLISH
THE CITY OF _____ PLANNING ORGANIZATION

Pursuant to authority granted by Section 160A-361 of the General Statutes of North Carolina *[and (citations of any special acts granting the city related authority)]*, the City Council enacts the following ordinance outlining the structure of its organization for planning and setting forth the responsibilities of certain components of that organization:

SECTION 1. Scope of Planning.
Every action and program of every component of the City of _____ involves planning, in a broad sense of the term. For purposes of this ordinance, the term is restricted to activities and programs involving physical, economic, and social development of the city.

SECTION 2. Planning Agencies.
The following are designated as planning agencies assigned responsibilities under this ordinance: the City Council, the Planning Board, the Planning Department, the Department of Community Development, the Inspection Department, the Zoning Board of Adjustment, the Housing Appeals Board, the Airport Zoning Board of Appeals, the Historic District Commission, the Historic Properties Commission, the Appearance Commission, the Redevelopment Commission, the Housing Authority, and the Economic Development Commission.[1]

SECTION 3. City Council.
In its legislative capacity the City Council adopts policies, ordinances, and amendments; appropriates funds; approves acquisition, construction, and disposition of public facilities; and oversees administration of the city. In its

---

[1]The list includes major entities authorized by the General Statutes. If the city does not have one or more of these, it should not include them in the list. If it has other agencies that it wishes to treat as planning agencies, it should add them to the list. If it has assigned different names to some of the agencies, it should use those names rather than the ones here.

quasi-judicial or administrative capacity, it *[issues (special-use permits) (conditional-use permits) under the zoning ordinance (G.S. 160A-381)], [gives final approval to plats of proposed subdivisions (G.S. 160A-373)], [approves redevelopment plans (G.S. 160 A-513)], [serves as a redevelopment commission (G.S. 160A-456, 160A-505)], [serves as a housing authority (G.S. 160A-456, 157-4.1)].*

SECTION 4. City Planning Board.[2]

The City Planning Board of the City of _____ is hereby created, in accordance with the following provisions.

A. Membership and Vacancies.

The Planning Board shall consist of _____ members. _____ members shall be citizens and residents of the City of _____ and shall be appointed by the City Council. _____ members shall be citizens and residents of the extraterritorial area described in an ordinance adopted _____ pursuant to G.S. 160A-360 and recorded in the Registry of Deeds of _____ County; such members shall be appointed by the _____ County Board of Commissioners pursuant to G.S. 160A-362. _____ of the initial members shall be appointed for a term of one year; _____, for two years; and _____, for three years. Their successors shall be appointed for terms of three years. Vacancies occurring for reasons other than expiration of terms shall be filled as they occur for the period of the unexpired term. Members may be removed for cause by the City Council.

B. Organization, Rules, Meetings, and Records.

Within thirty days after appointment the Planning Board shall meet and elect a chair and create and fill such offices as it may determine. The term of the chair and other officers shall be one year, with eligibility for reelection. The Board shall adopt rules for transaction of its business and shall keep a record of its members' attendance and of its resolutions, discussions, findings, and recommendations, which shall be a public record. The Board shall hold at least one meeting monthly, and all of its meetings shall be open to the public. There shall be a quorum of _____ members for the purpose of taking any official action.

C. General Powers and Duties.

It shall be the duty of the Planning Board, in general—

(1) To acquire and maintain in current form such basic information and materials as are necessary to an understanding of past trends, present conditions, and forces at work to cause changes in these conditions;

(2) To identify needs and problems growing out of those needs;

(3) To determine objectives to be sought in development of the area;

(4) To establish principles and policies for guiding action in development of the area;

---

[2]If there is no existing planning board, provisions such as those in Section 4 should be included in the ordinance. If a planning board is already in existence, language such as the following will be sufficient: *The _____ Planning Board created pursuant to an ordinance dated _____ shall continue to be constituted and to exercise powers and duties as directed by that ordinance.*

(5) To prepare and from time to time amend and revise a comprehensive and coordinated plan for the physical, social, and economic development of the area;

(6) To prepare and recommend to the City Council ordinances promoting orderly development along lines indicated in the comprehensive plan and advise it concerning proposed amendments of such ordinances;

(7) To determine whether specific proposed developments conform to the principles and requirements of the comprehensive plan for the growth and improvement of the area and ordinances adopted in furtherance of such plan;

(8) To keep the City Council and the general public informed and advised as to these matters; and

(9) To perform any other duties that may lawfully be assigned to it.

D. Basic Studies.

As background for its comprehensive plan and any ordinances it may prepare, the Planning Board may gather maps and aerial photographs of physical features of the area; statistics on past trends and present conditions with respect to population, property values, the economic base of the area, and land use; and such other information as is important or likely to be important in determining the amount, direction, and kind of development to be expected in the area and its various parts.

In addition, the Planning Board may make, cause to be made, or obtain special studies on the location, the condition, and the adequacy of specific facilities, which may include, but are not limited to, studies of housing; commercial and industrial facilities; parks, playgrounds, and other recreational facilities; public and private utilities; and traffic, transportation, and parking facilities.

All city officials shall, upon request, furnish to the Planning Board such available records or information as it may require in its work. The Board or its agents may, in the performance of its official duties, enter upon lands and make examinations or surveys and maintain necessary monuments thereon.

E. Comprehensive Plan.

The comprehensive plan, with the accompanying maps, plats, charts, and descriptive matter, shall be and show the Planning Board's recommendations to the City Council for the development of said territory, including, among other things, the general location, character, and extent of streets, bridges, boulevards, parkways, playgrounds, squares, parks, aviation fields, and other public ways, grounds, and open spaces; the general location and extent of public utilities and terminals, whether publicly or privately owned or operated, for water, light, sanitation, transportation, communication, power, and other purposes; the removal, relocation, widening, narrowing, vacating, abandonment, change of use, or extension of any of the foregoing ways, buildings, grounds, open spaces, property, utilities, or terminals; and the most desirable pattern of land use within the area, including areas for farming and forestry, for manufacturing and industrial uses, for commercial uses, for recreational uses, for open spaces, and for mixed uses.

The plan and any ordinances or other measures to effectuate it shall be made with the general purpose of guiding and accomplishing a coordinated, adjusted, and harmonious development of the city and its environs that will, in accordance with present and future needs, best promote health, safety, morals, and the general welfare, as well as efficiency and economy in the process of development; including, among other things, adequate provision for traffic, the promotion of safety from fire and other dangers, adequate provision for light and air, the promotion of the healthful and convenient distribution of population, the promotion of good civic design and arrangement, wise and efficient expenditure of public funds, and the adequate provision of public utilities, services, and other public requirements.

F. Subdivision Regulations.

The Planning Board shall prepare and submit to the City Council for its consideration and possible adoption regulations controlling the subdivision of land in accordance with the provisions of Part 2 of Article 19 of Chapter 160A of the General Statutes as amended. It shall review, from time to time, the effectiveness of such regulations and may make proposals to the City Council for amendment or other improvement of those regulations and their enforcement.

In accordance with the provisions of any regulations that are adopted, the Planning Board may review subdivision plats that are submitted and (a) make recommendations to the City Council concerning such plats or (b) approve, approve subject to conditions, or deny approval for the plat.

G. Zoning Ordinance.

The Planning Board shall prepare and submit to the City Council for its consideration and possible adoption a zoning ordinance in accordance with the provisions of Part 3 of Article 19 of Chapter 160A of the General Statutes as amended.

The Planning Board may initiate, from time to time, proposals for amendment of the zoning ordinance, based upon its studies and comprehensive plan. In addition, it shall review and make recommendations to the City Council concerning all proposed amendments to the zoning ordinance.

[The Planning Board shall serve as a Board of Adjustment under the zoning ordinance, hearing appeals, interpreting the ordinance, issuing or denying (special-use permits) (conditional-use permits), and granting variances.]

[The Planning Board shall act as a Board of Adjustment under the zoning ordinance in considering applications for and issuing or denying (special-use permits) (conditional-use permits) as authorized by that ordinance.]

H. Public Facilities.

The Planning Board shall review with the City Manager and other city officials and report its recommendations to the City Council concerning the location, extent, and design of all proposed public structures and facilities; the acquisition and disposition of public properties; and the establishment of building lines, mapped street lines, and proposals to change existing street lines. It shall also make recommendations concerning other matters referred to it by the City Council.

I. Historic *[Districts][Properties]*

[The Planning Board shall exercise the functions of a Historic District Commission, as authorized by Section 160A-396 of Article 3A of Chapter 160A of the General Statutes.]

[The Planning Board shall exercise the functions of a Historic Properties Commission, as authorized by Section 160A-399.2 of Article 3B of Chapter 160A of the General Statutes.]

[J. Urban Renewal.

The Planning Board shall make findings and recommendations concerning urban renewal projects in the area, as provided by Article 22 of Chapter 160A of the General Statutes.]

[K. Economic Development.

The Planning Board shall prepare and amend from time to time an economic development program for submission to the Economic Development Commission, as authorized by Section 158-13 of the General Statutes.]

L. Miscellaneous Powers and Duties.

The Planning Board may conduct such public hearings as may be required to gather information for the drafting, establishment, and maintenance of the comprehensive plan. Before adopting any such plan, it shall hold at least one public hearing thereon.

The Planning Board shall have power to promote public interest in and an understanding of its recommendations, and to that end it may publish and distribute copies of its recommendations and may employ such other means of publicity and education as it may elect.

Members or employees of the Planning Board, when duly authorized by the *[(Board) (City Manager) (City Council)]*, may attend planning conferences, meetings of planning associations, or hearings on pending planning legislation, and the Planning Board may *[by formal and affirmative vote]* authorize payment within the Board's budget of the reasonable traveling expenses incident to such attendance.

M. Annual Report and Budget Request.

The Planning Board shall, in May of each year, submit in writing to the City Council a report of its activities, an analysis of its expenditures to date for the current fiscal year, and its requested budget of funds needed for operation during the ensuing fiscal year.

[The Planning Board is authorized to receive contributions from private agencies, organizations, and individuals, in addition to any funds that may be appropriated for its use by the City Council. It may accept and disburse such contributions for special purposes or projects, subject to any specified conditions that it deems acceptable, whether or not such projects are included in the approved budget.]

N. Advisory Council and Special Committees.

The Planning Board may establish an unofficial Advisory Council and may cooperate with that Council to the end that its investigations and plans may receive full consideration, but the Board may not delegate to such Advisory Council any of its official powers and duties.

The Planning Board may from time to time establish special committees to assist it in studying specific questions and problems.

SECTION 5. Planning Department.

Under the direction of the City Manager, the Planning Department shall assist the City Council, the Planning Board, the Department of Community Development, the Inspection Department, the Zoning Board of Adjustment, the Housing Appeals Board, the Airport Zoning Board of Appeals, the Historic District Commission, the Historic Properties Commission, the Appearance Commission, the Redevelopment Commission, the Housing Authority, and the Economic Development Commission with studies, advice, and preparation of plans.[3]

SECTION 6. Department of Community Development.

The Department of Community Development formulates and carries out community development programs pursuant to Part 8 of Article 19 of Chapter 160A of the General Statutes.[4]

SECTION 7. Inspection Department.

The Inspection Department carries out the responsibilities set forth in Part 5 of Article 19 of Chapter 160A of the General Statutes with regard to enforcement of the State Building Code and other laws relating to construction. In addition, it enforces the minimum-housing-standards ordinance, the zoning ordinance, the sign ordinance, and other ordinances as assigned by the City Council and the Manager. Normally it is responsible for issuing permits, making inspections of both new construction and existing structures, issuing certificates of compliance, issuing orders to correct violations, initiating legal actions against violators, and keeping records.

SECTION 8. Zoning Board of Adjustment.

The Zoning Board of Adjustment is charged with hearing appeals from the Zoning Administrator's decisions; granting in specified circumstances special exceptions, special-use permits, or conditional-use permits under the zoning ordinance; and issuing variances under the zoning ordinance, all pursuant to provisions of Part 3 of Article 19 of Chapter 160A of the General Statutes and the zoning ordinance.

[The Board of Adjustment also serves as an Airport Zoning Board of Appeals, under the provisions of G.S. 63-33.]

---

[3]Any agencies not present in the particular city should be struck from the list.

[4]In some cities the department of community development includes a planning division, an inspections division, and support staffs for the historic district commission, the appearance commission, and perhaps other local boards.

[The Board of Adjustment also serves as a Housing Appeals Board with reference to the minimum-housing-standards ordinance, under the provisions of G.S. 160A-446.]

SECTION 9. Housing Appeals Board.

The Housing Appeals Board hears appeals under the minimum-housing-standards ordinance, pursuant to G.S. 160A-446.

SECTION 10. Airport Zoning Board of Appeals.

The Airport Zoning Board of Appeals hears appeals under the airport zoning ordinance, pursuant to G.S. 63-33.

SECTION 11. Historic District Commission.

Within historic districts established pursuant to Part 3A of Article 19 of Chapter 160A of the General Statutes, the Historic District Commission issues certificates of appropriateness for any changes of appearance of structures and seeks alternative uses for buildings proposed for demolition.

[The Historic District Commission also serves as a Historic Properties Commission with reference to such properties outside the historic district, pursuant to G.S. 160A-399.2.]

SECTION 12. Historic Properties Commission.

The Historic Properties Commission recommends properties to be designated as historic properties, acquires and manages such properties, conducts educational programs, issues certificates of appropriateness for changes in appearance of historic properties, and seeks alternative uses for historic properties proposed for demolition, all pursuant to Part 3B of Article 19 of Chapter 160A of the General Statutes.

[The Historic Properties Commission also serves as a Historic District Commission, pursuant to G.S. 160A-396.]

SECTION 13. Appearance Commission.

The Appearance Commission develops and carries out voluntary programs, policies, and ordinances to improve community appearance and advises governmental agencies on aesthetic matters, pursuant to Part 7 of Article 19 of Chapter 160A of the General Statutes.

[The Appearance Commission also serves as a Historic District Commission, pursuant to G.S. 160A-396.]

SECTION 14. Redevelopment Commission.

The Redevelopment Commission develops and carries out redevelopment projects, pursuant to Article 22 of Chapter 160A of the General Statutes.

[The Redevelopment Commission operates community development programs, pursuant to G.S. 160A-456.]

[The Redevelopment Commission acts as a Housing Authority, pursuant to G.S. 157-4.1.]

SECTION 15. Housing Authority.

The Housing Authority develops, carries out, and operates public housing programs and projects under Chapter 157 of the General Statutes.

[The Housing Authority operates community development programs, pursuant to G.S. 160A-456.]

[The Housing Authority acts as a Redevelopment Commission, pursuant to G.S. 160A-505.]

SECTION 16. Economic Development Commission.

The Economic Development Commission formulates economic development projects and promotes economic development of the area, pursuant to Article 2 of Chapter 158 of the General Statutes.

B

County Planning Organization Ordinance

AN ORDINANCE TO ESTABLISH
THE _____ COUNTY PLANNING ORGANIZATION

Pursuant to authority granted by Section 153A-321 of the General Statutes of North Carolina *[and (citations of any special acts granting the county related authority)]*, the Board of County Commissioners enacts the following ordinance outlining the structure of its organization for planning and setting forth the responsibilities of certain components of that organization:

SECTION 1. Scope of Planning.
Every action and program of every component of _____ County involves planning, in a broad sense of the term. For purposes of this ordinance, the term is restricted to activities and programs involving physical, economic, and social development of the county.

SECTION 2. Planning Agencies.
The following are designated as planning agencies assigned responsibilities under this ordinance: the Board of County Commissioners, the Planning Board, the Planning Department, the Department of Community Development, the Inspection Department, the Zoning Board of Adjustment, the Housing Appeals Board, the Airport Zoning Board of Appeals, the Historic District Commission, the Historic Properties Commission, the Appearance Commission, the Redevelopment Commission, the Housing Authority, and the Economic Development Commission.[1]

SECTION 3. Board of County Commissioners.
In its legislative capacity the Board adopts policies, ordinances, and amendments; appropriates funds; approves acquisition, construction, and disposition of public facilities; and oversees administration of the county. In its

---

[1]The list includes major entities authorized by the General Statutes. If the county does not have one or more of these, it should not include them in the list. If it has other agencies that it wishes to treat as planning agencies, it should add them to the list. If it has assigned different names to some of the agencies, it should use those names rather than the ones here.

quasi-judicial or administrative capacity, it *[issues (special-use permits) (conditional-use permits) under the zoning ordinance (G.S. 153A-340)], [gives final approval to plats of proposed subdivisions (G.S. 153A-332)], [approves redevelopment plans (G.S. 160 A-513)], [serves as a redevelopment commission (G.S. 153A-376, 160A-505)], [serves as a housing authority (G.S. 153A-376, 157-34)].*

SECTION 4. County Planning Board.[2]

The Planning Board of _____ County is hereby created, in accordance with the following provisions.

A. Membership and Vacancies.

The Planning Board shall consist of _____ members. All members shall be citizens and residents of _____ County and shall be appointed by the County Commissioners. _____ of the initial members shall be appointed for a term of one year; _____, for two years; and _____, for three years. Their successors shall be appointed for terms of three years. Vacancies occurring for reasons other than expiration of terms shall be filled as they occur for the period of the unexpired term. Members may be removed for cause by the County Commissioners.

B. Organization, Rules, Meetings, and Records.

Within thirty days after appointment the Planning Board shall meet and elect a chair and create and fill such offices as it may determine. The term of the chair and other officers shall be one year, with eligibility for reelection. The Board shall adopt rules for transaction of its business and shall keep a record of its members' attendance and of its resolutions, discussions, findings, and recommendations, which shall be a public record. The Board shall hold at least one meeting monthly, and all of its meetings shall be open to the public. There shall be a quorum of _____ members for the purpose of taking any official action.

C. General Powers and Duties.

It shall be the duty of the Planning Board, in general—

(1) To acquire and maintain in current form such basic information and materials as are necessary to an understanding of past trends, present conditions, and forces at work to cause changes in these conditions;

(2) To identify needs and problems growing out of those needs;

(3) To determine objectives to be sought in development of the area;

(4) To establish principles and policies for guiding action in development of the area;

(5) To prepare and from time to time amend and revise a comprehensive and coordinated plan for the physical, social, and economic development of the area;

---

[2]If there is no existing planning board, provisions such as those in Section 4 should be included in the ordinance. If a planning board is already in existence, language such as the following will be sufficient: *The _____ Planning Board created pursuant to an ordinance dated _____ shall continue to be constituted and to exercise powers and duties as directed by that ordinance.*

(6) To prepare and recommend to the County Commissioners ordinances promoting orderly development along lines indicated in the comprehensive plan and advise them concerning proposed amendments of such ordinances;

(7) To determine whether specific proposed developments conform to the principles and requirements of the comprehensive plan for the growth and improvement of the area and ordinances adopted in furtherance of such plan;

(8) To keep the County Commissioners and the general public informed and advised as to these matters; and

(9) To perform any other duties that may lawfully be assigned to it.

D. Basic Studies.

As background for its comprehensive plan and any ordinances it may prepare, the Planning Board may gather maps and aerial photographs of physical features of the area; statistics on past trends and present conditions with respect to population, property values, the economic base of the area, and land use; and such other information as is important or likely to be important in determining the amount, direction, and kind of development to be expected in the area and its various parts.

In addition, the Planning Board may make, cause to be made, or obtain special studies on the location, the condition, and the adequacy of specific facilities, which may include, but are not limited to, studies of housing; commercial and industrial facilities; parks, playgrounds, and other recreational facilities; public and private utilities; and traffic, transportation, and parking facilities.

All county officials shall, upon request, furnish to the Planning Board such available records or information as it may require in its work. The Board or its agents may, in the performance of its official duties, enter upon lands and make examinations or surveys and maintain necessary monuments thereon.

E. Comprehensive Plan.

The comprehensive plan, with the accompanying maps, plats, charts, and descriptive matter, shall be and show the Planning Board's recommendations to the County Commissioners for the development of said territory, including, among other things, the general location, character, and extent of streets, bridges, boulevards, parkways, playgrounds, squares, parks, aviation fields, and other public ways, grounds, and open spaces; the general location and extent of public utilities and terminals, whether publicly or privately owned or operated, for water, light, sanitation, transportation, communication, power, and other purposes; the removal, relocation, widening, narrowing, vacating, abandonment, change of use, or extension of any of the foregoing ways, buildings, grounds, open spaces, property, utilities, or terminals; and the most desirable pattern of land use within the area, including areas for farming and forestry, for manufacturing and industrial uses, for commercial uses, for recreational uses, for open spaces, and for mixed uses.

The plan and any ordinances or other measures to effectuate it shall be made with the general purpose of guiding and accomplishing a coordinated, adjusted, and harmonious development of the county that will, in accordance with present and future needs, best promote health, safety, morals, and the general welfare, as well as efficiency and economy in the process of development; including, among other things, adequate provision for traffic, the promotion of safety from fire and other dangers, adequate provision for light and air, the promotion of the healthful and convenient distribution of population, the promotion of good civic design and arrangement, wise and efficient expenditure of public funds, and the adequate provision of public utilities, services, and other public requirements.

F. Subdivision Regulations.

The Planning Board shall prepare and submit to the County Commissioners for their consideration and possible adoption regulations controlling the subdivision of land in accordance with the provisions of Part 2 of Article 18 of Chapter 153A of the General Statutes as amended. It shall review, from time to time, the effectiveness of such regulations and may make proposals to the County Commissioners for amendment or other improvement of those regulations and their enforcement.

In accordance with the provisions of any regulations that are adopted, the Planning Board may review subdivision plats that are submitted and (a) make recommendations to the County Commissioners concerning such plats or (b) approve, approve subject to conditions, or deny approval for the plat.

G. Zoning Ordinance.

The Planning Board shall prepare and submit to the County Commissioners for their consideration and possible adoption a zoning ordinance in accordance with the provisions of Part 3 of Article 18 of Chapter 153A of the General Statutes as amended.

The Planning Board may initiate, from time to time, proposals for amendment of the zoning ordinance, based upon its studies and comprehensive plan. In addition, it shall review and make recommendations to the County Commissioners concerning all proposed amendments to the zoning ordinance.

[The Planning Board shall serve as a Board of Adjustment under the zoning ordinance, hearing appeals, interpreting the ordinance, issuing or denying (special-use permits) (conditional-use permits), and granting variances.]

[The Planning Board shall act as a Board of Adjustment under the zoning ordinance in considering applications for and issuing or denying (special-use permits) (conditional-use permits) as authorized by that ordinance.]

H. Public Facilities.

The Planning Board shall review with the County Manager and other officials and report its recommendations to the County Commissioners concerning the location, extent, and design of all proposed public structures and facilities; the acquisition and disposition of public properties; and the establishment of building lines, mapped street lines, and proposals to change existing street lines. It shall also make recommendations concerning other matters referred to it by the County Commissioners.

I. Historic *[Districts][Properties]*

[The Planning Board shall exercise the functions of a Historic District Commission, as authorized by Section 160A-396 of Article 3A of Chapter 160A of the General Statutes.]

[The Planning Board shall exercise the functions of a Historic Properties Commission, as authorized by Section 160A-399.2 of Article 3B of Chapter 160A of the General Statutes.]

[J. Urban Renewal.

The Planning Board shall make findings and recommendations concerning urban renewal projects in the area, as provided by Article 22 of Chapter 160A of the General Statutes.]

[K. Economic Development.

The Planning Board shall prepare and amend from time to time an economic development program for submission to the Economic Development Commission, as authorized by Section 158-13 of the General Statutes.]

L. Miscellaneous Powers and Duties.

The Planning Board may conduct such public hearings as may be required to gather information for the drafting, establishment, and maintenance of the comprehensive plan. Before adopting any such plan, it shall hold at least one public hearing thereon.

The Planning Board shall have power to promote public interest in and an understanding of its recommendations, and to that end it may publish and distribute copies of its recommendations and may employ such other means of publicity and education as it may elect.

Members or employees of the Planning Board, when duly authorized by the *[(Board) (County Manager) (County Commissioners)]*, may attend planning conferences, meetings of planning associations, or hearings on pending planning legislation, and the Planning Board may *[by formal and affirmative vote]* authorize payment within the Board's budget of the reasonable traveling expenses incident to such attendance.

M. Annual Report and Budget Request.

The Planning Board shall, in May of each year, submit in writing to the County Commissioners a report of its activities, an analysis of its expenditures to date for the current fiscal year, and its requested budget of funds needed for operation during the ensuing fiscal year.

[The Planning Board is authorized to receive contributions from private agencies, organizations, and individuals, in addition to any funds that may be appropriated for its use by the County Commissioners. It may accept and disburse such contributions for special purposes or projects, subject to any specified conditions that it deems acceptable, whether or not such projects are included in the approved budget.]

N. Advisory Council and Special Committees.

The Planning Board may establish an unofficial Advisory Council and may cooperate with that Council to the end that its investigations and plans may receive full consideration, but the Board may not delegate to such Advisory Council any of its official powers and duties.

The Planning Board may from time to time establish special committees to assist it in studying specific questions and problems.

SECTION 5. Planning Department.

Under the direction of the County Manager, the Planning Department shall assist the County Commissioners, the Planning Board, the Department of Community Development, the Inspection Department, the Zoning Board of Adjustment, the Housing Appeals Board, the Airport Zoning Board of Appeals, the Historic District Commission, the Historic Properties Commission, the Appearance Commission, the Redevelopment Commission, the Housing Authority, and the Economic Development Commission with studies, advice, and preparation of plans.[3]

SECTION 6. Department of Community Development.

The Department of Community Development formulates and carries out community development programs pursuant to Part 5 of Article 18 of Chapter 153A of the General Statutes.[4]

SECTION 7. Inspection Department.

The Inspection Department carries out the responsibilities set forth in Part 4 of Article 18 of Chapter 153A of the General Statutes with regard to enforcement of the State Building Code and other laws relating to construction. In addition, it enforces the minimum-housing-standards ordinance, the zoning ordinance, the sign ordinance, and other ordinances as assigned by the County Commissioners and the Manager. Normally it is responsible for issuing permits, making inspections of both new construction and existing structures, issuing certificates of compliance, issuing orders to correct violations, initiating legal actions against violators, and keeping records.

SECTION 8. Zoning Board of Adjustment.

The Zoning Board of Adjustment is charged with hearing appeals from the Zoning Administrator's decisions; granting in specified circumstances special exceptions, special-use permits, or conditional-use permits under the zoning ordinance; and issuing variances under the zoning ordinance, all pursuant to provisions of Part 3 of Article 18 of Chapter 153A of the General Statutes and the zoning ordinance.

[The Board of Adjustment also serves as an Airport Zoning Board of Appeals, under the provisions of G.S. 63-33.]

---

[3]Any agencies not present in the particular county should be struck from the list.

[4]In some counties the department of community development includes a planning division, an inspections division, and support staffs for the historic district commission, the appearance commission, and perhaps other local boards.

[The Board of Adjustment also serves as a Housing Appeals Board with reference to the minimum-housing-standards ordinance, under the provisions of G.S. 160A-446.]

SECTION 9. Housing Appeals Board.

The Housing Appeals Board hears appeals under the minimum-housing-standards ordinance, pursuant to G.S. 160A-446.

SECTION 10. Airport Zoning Board of Appeals.

The Airport Zoning Board of Appeals hears appeals under the airport zoning ordinance, pursuant to G.S. 63-33.

SECTION 11. Historic District Commission.

Within historic districts established pursuant to Part 3A of Article 19 of Chapter 160A of the General Statutes, the Historic District Commission issues certificates of appropriateness for any changes of appearance of structures and seeks alternative uses for buildings proposed for demolition.

[The Historic District Commission also serves as a Historic Properties Commission with reference to such properties outside the historic district, pursuant to G.S. 160A-399.2.]

SECTION 12. Historic Properties Commission.

The Historic Properties Commission recommends properties to be designated as historic properties, acquires and manages such properties, conducts educational programs, issues certificates of appropriateness for changes in appearance of historic properties, and seeks alternative uses for historic properties proposed for demolition, all pursuant to Part 3B of Article 19 of Chapter 160A of the General Statutes.

[The Historic Properties Commission also serves as a Historic District Commission, pursuant to G.S. 160A-396.]

SECTION 13. Appearance Commission.

The Appearance Commission develops and carries out voluntary programs, policies, and ordinances to improve community appearance and advises governmental agencies on aesthetic matters, pursuant to Part 7 of Article 19 of Chapter 160A of the General Statutes.

[The Appearance Commission also serves as a Historic District Commission, pursuant to G.S. 160A-396.]

SECTION 14. Redevelopment Commission.

The Redevelopment Commission develops and carries out redevelopment projects pursuant to Article 22 of Chapter 160A of the General Statutes.

[The Redevelopment Commission operates community development programs, pursuant to G.S. 153A-376.]

[The Redevelopment Commission acts as a Housing Authority, pursuant to G.S. 157-4.1.]

SECTION 15. Housing Authority.

The Housing Authority develops, carries out, and operates public housing programs and projects under Chapter 157 of the General Statutes.

[The Housing Authority operates community development programs, pursuant to G.S. 153A-376.]

[The Housing Authority acts as a Redevelopment Commission, pursuant to G.S. 160A-505.]

SECTION 16. Economic Development Commission.

The Economic Development Commission formulates economic development projects and promotes economic development of the area, pursuant to Article 2 of Chapter 158 of the General Statutes.

Agreement Creating a Joint City-County Planning Board

ORDINANCE AND RESOLUTION ESTABLISHING CHARLOTTE-MECKLENBURG PLANNING COMMISSION

BE IT ORDAINED AND RESOLVED BY THE CITY COUNCIL OF CHARLOTTE AND THE BOARD OF COUNTY COMMISSIONERS OF MECKLENBURG COUNTY:

SECTION 1. Finding and Declaration of Necessity.

The City Council of the City of Charlotte and Board of County Commissioners of Mecklenburg County, herein called "Governing Bodies," hereby find and declare that it is a governmental necessity that a planning board be established and maintained in Mecklenburg County, including the City of Charlotte, pursuant to the provisions of General Statutes, Section 160-22 through 160-24,[1] and that the expense of same will be necessary expense. Without limiting the generality of the foregoing it is especially declared and found that plans, investigations, surveys and recommendations by such a board are necessary in order that the officers, agents, employees, and governing bodies may competently perform their duties and in order that the voters of the City of Charlotte and/or Mecklenburg County, when called on to exercise their franchise in elections relating to the affairs of the City of Charlotte and/or Mecklenburg County may do so with an intelligent understanding of the questions presented for their decisions.

SECTION 2. Establishment of Planning Board, Duties.

There is hereby established a board to be known as the Charlotte-Mecklenburg Planning Commission. Its duties shall be to make careful study of the resources, possibilities and needs of the city, particularly with respect to conditions which may be injurious to the public welfare or otherwise injurious and to make plans for the development of Mecklenburg County, including the City of Charlotte, but excluding all incorporated towns in

---

[1]Now Part 1, Article 20, of Chapter 160A.

Mecklenburg County other than the City of Charlotte. In connection with the performance of its duties the board shall make or cause to be made such surveys, investigations and compilations of facts as it may deem useful or necessary. Among other things it shall from time to time consider the desirability of the extension of the limits of the City of Charlotte, and if it finds such extension to be desirable, it shall prepare and present to the City Council a program of extension with a statement of the reasons for the same. The City Council shall not, nor shall any official of the city, approve any subdivision development which is subject to the jurisdiction of the City without first presenting the same to the Board and receiving its recommendations with respect thereto. From time to time and at least once each year, the Board shall report to the governing bodies, giving information regarding the condition of Mecklenburg County, including the City of Charlotte, and present any plans or proposals for the development of Mecklenburg County, including the City of Charlotte, which it desires to submit together with estimates of the cost of the same.

SECTION 3. Qualifications for Membership, Terms of Office.

The Board shall consist of ten (10) members, all of whom shall be residents of Mecklenburg County, North Carolina, and in addition thereto, two ex officio members who shall be the City Manager of the City of Charlotte and the Chairman of the Board of County Commissioners of Mecklenburg County. The ex officio members shall serve in an advisory capacity only and shall not have a vote and shall only attend such meetings to which they are especially invited. Five (5) members of such Board shall be appointed by the City Council of the City of Charlotte, and the other five members of such Board shall be appointed by the Board of County Commissioners of Mecklenburg County. For the first board each governing body shall appoint one member whose term will end June 30, 1955, two members whose terms will end June 30, 1956, and two members whose terms will end June 30, 1957. Thereafter the terms of all members appointed by each governing body shall be three years except that in case of a vacancy occurring during a term the same shall be filled by the governing body having authority to make such appointment for the unexpired portion of such term.

Any appointed member of the Board may be removed at any time with or without cause by a two-thirds vote of the governing body having authority to appoint such member's successor.

The members of such Board shall serve without pay.

SECTION 4. Organization, Officers, Rules, Meetings.

The first board shall meet for the purpose of organization as soon as reasonably possible after its creation on joint call from the Mayor of the City of Charlotte and Chairman of the Board of County Commissioners. The Board shall elect its own officers and shall adopt such rules as it shall see fit for the transaction of its business. A copy of such rules shall be filed with the

City Clerk of the City of Charlotte and with the Auditor of Mecklenburg County for inspection by interested parties and shall constitute public records. The board shall hold regular meetings and the same shall be open to the public, but this shall not prevent the board when it sees fit from the holding of executive sessions.[2] The board shall invite and receive suggestions from the public concerning any and all matters within the scope of its duties. It shall keep minutes of its meetings, in which shall be recorded all actions taken by it on all matters that it considers. Such minutes shall be public records.

SECTION 5. Budgets.

As soon as reasonably possible after its organization, the first board shall prepare and present to each governing body an estimate of its monetary requirements until the end of the current fiscal year, showing in detail the various purposes for which the money will be needed. The governing bodies, after making such modifications as they see fit, shall approve the budget for the board until the end of the current fiscal year and shall from funds currently appropriated for planning purposes as shall be approved at joint meetings of the governing bodies, appropriate funds sufficient to meet such budget. Thereafter the board shall annually file with the City Manager and the Chairman of the County Board of Commissioners, an estimate of its requirements for the ensuing fiscal year and such other information as such officials, or either of them, may need in connection with their presentation to the governing bodies of the budget estimate required by law.

Money appropriated to the board shall not be paid to it in a lump sum, but shall be disbursed as are other joint City-County funds and in accordance with the regular course and practices of the City of Charlotte and Mecklenburg County.

SECTION 6. Additional Municipalities Participating.

Provided, however, nothing hereinbefore set forth shall be construed to prohibit the inclusion of any municipality in Mecklenburg County from participating in the Charlotte-Mecklenburg Planning Commission and receiving the services herein provided, under such terms and regulations as may be provided by the appropriate legislative bodies.

---

[2]This provision should be altered to take account of the open meetings law, Article 33C of Chapter 143 of the General Statutes.

Agreement Creating a Joint Multicounty Planning Board

AGREEMENT BETWEEN THE COUNTY OF HALIFAX, THE COUNTY OF NORTHAMPTON, AND THE COUNTY OF WARREN FOR THE CREATION OF A JOINT PLANNING BOARD TO BE KNOWN AS THE LAKE GASTON REGIONAL PLANNING BOARD

THIS AGREEMENT entered into between the County of Halifax, the County of Northampton, and the County of Warren, on this the _____ day of _____, 1965:

WITNESSETH:

That for and in consideration of the mutual covenants herein set out and in consideration of the public needs and benefits accruing to the public welfare and to each of the parties hereto, and pursuant to Section 153-9 (40)[1] of the General Statutes of North Carolina as amended, the parties hereto do mutually agree as follows:

SECTION 1. Creation of the Lake Gaston Regional Planning Board.

There is hereby established a joint Planning Board to be known as "THE LAKE GASTON REGIONAL PLANNING BOARD" (hereinafter called the "Board").

SECTION 2. Membership.

The Board shall be composed of the chairman and members, *ex officio*, of the Halifax County Planning Board and the Halifax County Board of Commissioners; the chairman and members, *ex officio*, of the Northampton County Planning Board and the Northampton County Board of Commissioners; and the chairman and members, *ex officio*, of the Warren County Planning Board and the Warren County Board of Commissioners. All such members shall have duties as members of this Board in addition to the other duties of the offices which they hold, and membership on this Board shall not constitute an additional office. All members of this Board shall serve

---

[1]Now Article 19 of Chapter 153A.

without compensation; provided, however, that each member county may, in the discretion of its governing board, reimburse its members for their actual expenses incurred in performance of their duties as Board members.

SECTION 3. Organization, Officers, Rules, Meetings.

The Board shall meet initially on call of the Chairman of the Warren County Planning Board, who shall serve as temporary Chairman of the Board until his successor is elected, at a place and time (no later than October 1, 1965) designated by him, for the purpose of organization. The Board shall elect its own officers and shall adopt such rules as it shall see fit for the transaction of its business. The Board shall hold regular meetings at intervals no longer than once every three months, which meetings shall be open to the public. The Board shall keep minutes of its meetings, which shall constitute public records.

SECTION 4. Powers and Duties.

It shall be the duty of the Board to prepare plans and to coordinate the plans of their respective regional and county planning boards within the vicinity of Lake Gaston so as to bring about a better coordinated and more harmonious development of the Lake Gaston area. The Board shall be empowered:

(a) To acquire and maintain in current form such basic information and materials as are necessary to an understanding of past trends, present conditions, and forces at work to cause changes in these conditions;

(b) To prepare and from time to time amend and revise a comprehensive and coordinated plan for the physical development of the area; provided that in the preparation or amendment of such plan or plans the Board shall take account of and shall seek to harmonize its plan or plans with those of any other state, regional, or local planning agency within the Lake Gaston area;

(c) To establish principles and policies for guiding action in the development of the Lake Gaston area, and to recommend said policies or principles to the federal government or any agency thereof, to the appropriate state government or governments or any agency or agencies thereof, and to any local governing boards or agencies within the area;

(d) To prepare and recommend to the city and county governing boards in the Lake Gaston area ordinances promoting orderly development along the lines indicated in the comprehensive plan;

(e) To determine whether specific proposed developments referred to it by governmental or private agencies in the area conform to the principles and requirements of the comprehensive plan for the area, and to make appropriate recommendations to any appropriate governmental body or agency concerning them;

(f) To meet with and to coordinate its activities and programs with any other regional planning agency in the Lake Gaston area;

(g) To keep the appropriate federal, state, and city and county governments and agencies and the general public informed and advised upon any matter of concern related to the development of the Lake Gaston area;

(h) To make any other recommendations which it sees fit for improving or coordinating the development of the area; and

(i) To perform any other duties that may lawfully be assigned to it.

In carrying out such powers and duties, such Board:

(a) May, within the limits of any funds appropriated to it, given to it, or otherwise made available to it, appoint such employees and engage such consultants as it may require;

(b) May, within the limits of funds appropriated to it, given to it, or otherwise made available to it, acquire property and materials for its use and incur other necessary expenses;

(c) May authorize its agents or employees or members, in performance of their official duties, to enter upon lands and make examinations or surveys and maintain necessary monuments thereon;

(d) May perform any of the actions authorized for County Planning Boards by Section 153-9 (40)[2] of the General Statutes of North Carolina as amended; and

(e) Shall prepare an annual report for the parties to this agreement in April of each year.

SECTION 5. Effective Date.

This Agreement shall become effective when duly executed by the parties hereto.

IN WITNESS WHEREOF, the County of Halifax, the County of Northampton, and the County of Warren have caused this instrument to be executed by the Chairmen of their Boards of County Commissioners and attested by their Clerks and their corporate seals attached.

---

[2]Now Sections 153A-321 and 153A-322.

Agreement Creating a Regional Planning and Economic Development Commission

RESOLUTION AND AGREEMENT BETWEEN
THE COUNTY OF BEAUFORT, THE COUNTY OF EDGECOMBE,
THE COUNTY OF MARTIN, THE COUNTY OF NASH,
THE COUNTY OF PITT, AND THE COUNTY OF WILSON
FOR THE CREATION OF A COMMISSION TO BE KNOWN AS THE
COASTAL PLAIN PLANNING AND DEVELOPMENT COMMISSION

THIS AGREEMENT entered into between the County of Beaufort, the County of Edgecombe, the County of Martin, the County of Nash, the County of Pitt, and the County of Wilson on this _____ day of _____, 1962:

WITNESSETH:

That for and in consideration of the mutual covenants herein set out and in consideration of the public needs and of benefits accruing to the public welfare and to each of the parties hereto, and pursuant to Section 158-14 and Section 153-276[1] of the General Statutes of North Carolina as amended, the parties hereto do mutually agree as follows:

SECTION 1. Creation of the Coastal Plain Planning and Development Commission.

There is hereby established a Regional Planning and Economic Development Commission to be known as "THE COASTAL PLAIN PLANNING AND DEVELOPMENT COMMISSION" (hereinafter called the "Commission").

SECTION 2. Membership.

The Commission shall be composed of representatives designated by those governmental units in the Coastal Plain area which enter into this agreement. The initial membership shall consist of the Counties of Beaufort, Edgecombe, Martin, Nash, Pitt, and Wilson. Any incorporated municipality within these counties may also be admitted to membership, provided (a) that its governing board officially adopts this resolution and agreement and

---

[1]Now Section 153A-398.

(b) its application is officially approved by resolution of each of the existing parties to this agreement.

Each county holding membership on the Commission shall be entitled to three representatives. Each municipality whose population is greater than 20,000 shall be entitled to two representatives. Each municipality whose population is 20,000 or less shall be entitled to one representative.

Designation of Representatives. Unless a County Board of Commissioners adopts a resolution providing for another method of appointment, its representatives shall be designated as follows: The Chairman of the Board of County Commissioners shall serve as an *ex officio* representative, fulfilling this responsibility in addition to his other duties. The County Commissioners shall appoint one representative who is actively connected with the field of agriculture, after receiving and considering recommendations from any organized and active agricultural agencies and/or organizations within the county. The County Commissioners shall appoint one representative who is actively connected with the fields of commerce or industry, after receiving and considering recommendations from any organized and active economic development organizations within the county.

Unless a municipal governing board adopts a resolution providing for another method of appointment, its representatives shall be designated as follows: The Mayor of the municipality shall serve as an *ex officio* representative, fulfilling this responsibility in addition to his other duties. The second representative of any municipality over 20,000 population shall be appointed by the municipal governing board, after receiving and considering recommendations from any organized and active economic development organization serving the municipality.

No appointed representative shall be a person engaged professionally (either as a consultant or on a full-time basis) in furnishing advice, assistance, or other services to an organization or agency engaged in industrial, commercial, or agricultural development, or in urban or rural planning.

Ex officio representatives shall be entitled to vote and shall have and exercise all rights, privileges, responsibilities, and duties of other members, except in instances where this resolution and agreement expressly provide for different treatment.

All representatives shall be referred to hereafter in this resolution and agreement as "Commissioners."

Terms of Office. Ex officio Commissioners shall serve on the Commission only during their terms of office as Chairman of a County Board of Commissioners or as Mayor. One of the two Commissioners initially appointed by each county shall serve until January 1, 1964; the other shall serve until January 1, 1966; their successors shall be appointed for three-year terms. The Commissioner initially appointed by a municipality over 20,000 population shall serve for three years and until the January 1 which next follows the expiration of this period; his successors shall be appointed for three-year terms. Vacancies occurring for reasons other than the expiration of terms shall be filled by the appropriate appointive body for the period of the unexpired term. Commissioners shall continue in office until their successors shall have qualified and taken office. Commissioners shall be eligible for reappointment upon the expiration of their terms.

Conditions of Membership. Faithful attendance at meetings of the Commission and conscientious performance of the duties required of Commissioners shall be a prerequisite to continuing membership on the Commission. The governing body appointing any Commissioner shall have the authority to remove such Commissioner at any time for cause stated in writing and after hearing.

Compensation of Commissioners. Compensation or reimbursement of traveling and other expenses incurred in the performance of their duties shall be paid to Commissioners only in accordance with policies established in the Commission's rules and regulations and in accordance with the approved budget for the fiscal year.

SECTION 3. Organization of Commission.

First Meeting. The Commission shall meet within forty-five (45) days following the ratification of this agreement by the original parties to it, in the City of Greenville, on call of Senator Dallas L. Alford, Jr., the Chairman of the Steering Committee heretofore established, who shall preside until a Chairman has been elected. At this meeting the Commission shall elect, by a majority vote of the Commissioners present, a Chairman, a Vice-Chairman, and a Secretary. The terms of the original officers shall be until January 1, 1963. Thereafter terms of officers shall be for one year, with eligibility for re-election. The Commission shall adopt rules for the transaction of its business, and it shall keep a record of the Commissioners' attendance and of its resolutions, discussions, findings, and recommendations, which record shall be a public record. A majority of the Commissioners shall constitute a quorum for the purpose of taking any official action required by this resolution and agreement.

Meetings. Meetings of the Commission shall be held regularly at least once every three months, at places and on dates specified by the Commission. Special meetings may be called from time to time by the Chairman on his own initiative, and must be called by him at the request of five or more members of the Commission. All members shall be notified by the Chairman in writing of the time and place of all regular and special meetings at least five days in advance of such meeting. All meetings shall be open to the public.

Committees. The following committees shall be created by the Commission: (1) Planning Committee, (2) Youth Committee, (3) Agriculture Development Committee, (4) Industrial Development Committee, (5) Travel and Recreation Committee, (6) Committee on Education and Cultural Affairs, (7) Community Development Committee, (8) Finance Committee. Additional permanent or temporary committees may be established by the Commission as may be deemed necessary to assist in the study of specific questions and problems or the direction of specific programs or areas of work.

The chairman and vice-chairman of each of the named committees shall be Commissioners appointed by the Commission Chairman. Additional committee members may be appointed by the Commission Chairman from within or outside the Commission, as may be deemed necessary by the Chairman, with the approval of the Commission.

Staff. Within the limits of appropriated funds, the Commission may (1) hire and fix the compensation of such employees and staffs as it may deem necessary for its work; (2) contract with planners or other experts for such services as it may require; (3) contract with the State of North Carolina or the federal government, or any agency or department thereof, for such services as may be provided by such agencies, and carry out the provisions of such contract.

Office and Equipment. Within the limits of appropriated funds, the Commission may lease, rent, or purchase, or otherwise obtain suitable quarters and office space for its staff, and may lease, rent, or purchase necessary furniture, fixtures, and other equipment, and supplies.

SECTION 4. Fiscal Affairs.

Sources of Revenue. The Commission may accept, receive, and disburse in furtherance of its functions any funds, grants, and services made available by the federal government and its agencies, the state government and its agencies, any municipalities or counties, and by private and civic sources.

Budgetary Procedures. The Commission shall prepare each year a report of its activities, including a financial statement, and this report shall be distributed to all member counties and municipalities during the month of April. The Commission shall also adopt and file with each of the member counties and municipalities at this time a recommended budget for its operations for the fiscal year beginning the following July 1.

The recommended budget shall contain an estimate of all expenditures necessary to finance its operations in the budget year, in such detail as the Commission shall determine, and an estimate of all revenues from all sources that will be available to the Commission for such year. It shall also contain an estimate of the necessary appropriations to be made by the member counties and municipalities. The amount to be contributed by each member county or municipality shall be determined by dividing the total amount of such appropriations in the proportion that the population of such member county or municipality bears to the total population of all the member counties and municipalities, as said populations were enumerated in the past decennial census.

The recommended budget shall show separately the revenues and expenditures needed to finance planning operations under Article 23 of Chapter 153[2] of the General Statutes and economic development operations under Article 2 of Chapter 158 of the General Statutes.

---

[2]Now Article 19 of Chapter 153A.

The governing boards of the member counties and municipalities shall consider the recommended budget and have an opportunity to recommend changes to the Commission during the month of May. The Commission shall consider such recommendations and adopt a final budget in the first week of June each year. Copies of such budget shall immediately be distributed to member counties and municipalities. The budget so adopted shall be binding upon the Commission, and any amendment thereto shall be made only with the approval of the governing bodies of all member counties and municipalities. Funds from any source other than appropriations by the member counties and municipalities shall be budgeted in accordance with the rules and regulations or conditions imposed by the donor from whom such funds were received. Appropriations from each member county or municipality shall be according to the formula set forth heretofore. Each member county or municipality shall in its annual budget appropriate funds for payment of its contribution to the Commission.

Handling of Commission Funds. The Commission shall select a Treasurer, who may be but is not required to be a Commissioner, who shall furnish bond of a surety company authorized to do business in North Carolina in such amount as the Commission may require, which bond shall be approved by the Commission.

All funds received by or on behalf of the Commission shall be turned over to the Treasurer of the Commission, who shall give an appropriate receipt therefor.

The Commission is hereby authorized and empowered to select and designate, by recorded resolution, a bank or banks or trust company in this state as official depository or depositories of the funds of the Commission, which funds shall be secured in accordance with Section 159-28 of the General Statutes.

The Treasurer of the Commission shall daily deposit all funds of the Commission coming into his possession in the official depository or depositories, in such accounts as he shall deem necessary and appropriate. The Treasurer shall designate separate accounts for funds required to be used for planning operations and for funds required to be used for economic development operations.

No funds belonging to the Commission shall be expended except by check signed by the Treasurer and countersigned by the Chairman of the Commission. No expenditure of Commission funds shall be made until such expenditure shall have been approved by the Commission. No contract or agreement requiring the payment of money shall be made unless authorized by the Commission. No such contract or expenditure shall be authorized or approved by the Commission unless provision for payment thereof has been made in the Commission's budget as adopted by member counties and municipalities and unless the Commission shall determine that a sufficient unencumbered balance remains of such provision for payment of the obligation. All contracts and agreements requiring the payment of money shall be signed by the Chairman of the Commission and attested by the Secretary.

Accounts to be Kept. The Treasurer shall keep an account for each appropriation made in the budget of the Commission, showing in detail the amount appropriated thereto, the amount drawn therefrom, the unpaid obligations charged against it, and the unencumbered balance to the credit thereof. He shall keep a record of the date, source, and amount of each item or receipt, and the date, the payee or contractor, the specific purpose, and the amount of every disbursement or contract made. He shall also keep a copy of every contract made requiring the payment of money. The Treasurer shall keep separate sets of accounts, in accord with the above requirements, for appropriations, revenues, and expenditures made pursuant to Article 23 of Chapter 153[3] of the General Statutes and for appropriations, revenues, and expenditures made pursuant to Article 2 of Chapter 158 of the General Statutes.

Financial Reports. The Treasurer shall as often as may be required by the Commission file with it a statement of the financial condition of the Commission, showing its receipts and expenditures in detail.

The Commission shall, annually within 90 days following the end of the fiscal year, provide the governing body of each member county or municipality with an audit of its receipts and expenditures made by a certified public accountant; or alternately, it may at the direction of any member county or municipality governing board make its accounts available to the unit's regular auditing accountant for such audit at a reasonable time.

SECTION 5. Powers and Duties of the Commission.

The Commission shall have and exercise any or all of the powers and duties granted to a Regional Planning Commission by the provisions of Article 23 of Chapter 153[4] of the General Statutes and in particular as set forth in Section 153-280[5] of said article. In addition, the Commission shall have and exercise any or all of the powers and duties granted to a Regional Economic Development Commission by the provisions of Article 2 of Chapter 158 of the General Statutes and in particular as set forth in Section 158-13 of said article.

SECTION 6. Withdrawal of Member; Penalty for Non-Payment of Member's Annual Contribution.

Any member county or municipality may withdraw from membership in the Commission upon giving two years' written notice to the Commission and to the governing board of each of the other member counties and municipalities. Any member county or municipality failing to pay its annual contribution called for by the approved budget shall be suspended from

---

[3]Now Article 19 of Chapter 153A.
[4]Now Article 19 of Chapter 153A.
[5]Now Section 153A-395.

membership and its representatives denied the right to vote during the fiscal year for which such payment is due. Failure to contribute for two successive years shall constitute grounds for expulsion of the delinquent member county or municipality from the Commission, upon majority vote of all the Commissioners from the other member counties and municipalities.

SECTION 7. Modification, Amendment, and Repeal of this Resolution.

This resolution and agreement may be modified, amended, or repealed at any time, through action by the governing boards of all member counties and municipalities.

SECTION 8. Separability.

It is the intent of the parties to this resolution and agreement that should any provision of the General Statutes on which this resolution and agreement is based be declared by the courts to be unconstitutional or invalid for any reason, such decision will not affect the validity of the resolution and agreement as a whole or any part thereof other than the part so decided to be unconstitutional or invalid.

SECTION 9. Effective Date.

This resolution and agreement shall become effective on the date on which all parties named herein have duly adopted and executed it.

IN WITNESS WHEREOF, the County of Beaufort, the County of Edgecombe, the County of Martin, the County of Nash, the County of Pitt, and the County of Wilson have duly adopted this resolution and have caused this instrument to be executed by the Chairmen of the Boards of County Commissioners and attested by their Clerks and their corporate seals attached on the dates shown.

In witness whereof, the Commissioners of the County of _____, North Carolina, have caused this resolution and agreement to be executed by the Chairman of its Board of County Commissioners, approved by the County Attorney, and attested by the Clerk of said Board, and its corporate seal to be impressed thereon, this the _____ day of _____, 1962.

Agreement Creating a Regional Council of Local Officials

RESOLUTION PROVIDING FOR THE CREATION OF A REGIONAL COUNCIL OF LOCAL OFFICIALS TO BE KNOWN AS THE PIEDMONT TRIAD COUNCIL OF GOVERNMENTS AND TO BE COMPOSED OF ELECTED REPRESENTATIVES FROM THE FOLLOWING GOVERNMENTAL UNITS: THE COUNTY OF FORSYTH, THE COUNTY OF GUILFORD, THE CITY OF GREENSBORO, THE CITY OF HIGH POINT, AND THE CITY OF WINSTON-SALEM

WHEREAS, the 1967 Session of the North Carolina General Assembly enacted Chapter 797 of the 1967 Session Laws (G.S. 160-77.1 through 160-77.6)[1] authorizing any two or more municipalities and counties to create a regional council of local officials[2] with such powers as are specified in the creating resolution or any amendments thereto; and

WHEREAS, the governing bodies of the Counties of Guilford and Forsyth, and the Cities of High Point, Winston-Salem and Greensboro have expressed an interest in the creation of a regional council of local officials; and the Board of Commissioners of Forsyth County finds that it would be in the best interest of the citizens of this county for Forsyth County to join in the creation of such regional council of local officials; and

WHEREAS, a regional council of local officials would benefit the governmental units participating in such a council, would provide a forum in which the participating officials might study and discuss community problems of mutual interest and concern, and could lead to the making of recommendations for consideration by the participating local governing bodies;

NOW, THEREFORE, BE IT RESOLVED by the Board of Commissioners of Forsyth County that Forsyth County join with the Cities of Winston-Salem, Greensboro, and High Point, and the County of Guilford in the formation of a regional council of local officials, with the bylaws of said council being as follows:

---

[1]Now Part 2, Article 20, of G.S. Chapter 160A.
[2]Now regional council of governments.

BYLAWS OF THE PIEDMONT TRIAD COUNCIL OF GOVERNMENTS

ARTICLE I

SECTION 1. Name of Council.

The name of the regional council of local officials hereby created is the "Piedmont Triad Council of Governments." It is hereinafter referred to as the "Council."

SECTION 2. Membership.

(a) The members of the Council shall initially consist of one member from each of the governing bodies of the Cities of Greensboro, High Point, and Winston-Salem, and the Counties of Forsyth and Guilford. The governing bodies of other cities and counties may apply for membership in the Council. Upon approval of any such application by each governmental unit participating in the Council at the time such application is received, and upon adoption by the applicant of a resolution identical to the ones under which the Council is then operating, the governing body of the applicant shall select one of its members to be a member of the Council. Each member shall serve at the pleasure of the participating governmental unit by which such member is selected.

(b) Any participating governmental unit may withdraw from the Council at the end of any fiscal year, after having given sixty (60) days' notice to the other participating governmental units, by adopting a resolution to that effect and sending a certified copy of said resolution to the other participating governments.

SECTION 3. Purposes.

The purposes of the Council shall be:

(1) to serve as a forum for discussion of governmental problems of mutual interest and concern;

(2) to develop and formalize policy recommendations concerning matters having an area-wide significance;

(3) to promote inter-governmental cooperation;

(4) to provide organizational machinery to insure effective communication and coordination among participating governmental units;

(5) to serve as a vehicle for the collection and distribution of information concerning matters of area-wide interest; and

(6) to review upon request of a participating governmental unit applications of that unit for any grant in aid, federal, state or private.

The Council shall strive to promote harmony and cooperation among its members. It shall seek to deal with metropolitan problems in a manner which is mutually satisfactory, and shall respect the autonomy of all local governments within the Piedmont Triad area—which is defined as including the combined geographic areas of the participating governmental units.

SECTION 4. Finance Matters.

On or before the 15th day of April each year, the Council shall prepare and submit to each participating governmental unit a proposed budget for the next fiscal year commencing July 1. The budget shall be divided into two parts. Part A shall include all items which the Council shall have authority to expend without further approval of the participating governmental units. Part B shall include all items which the Council may not expend without further approval of the participating governmental units.

The budget shall also set out the proportionate share (in terms of percentage based upon the latest decennial census) of the budget to be borne by each participating governmental unit.

Upon approval of the budget by all participating governmental units, each participating governmental unit shall appropriate its share of the budget and shall forward to the Council Accountant its share of Part A of the budget. All such appropriations shall be made in accordance with the Municipal or County Fiscal Control Act, as may be appropriate. The Council may, with the agreement of the governing body involved, designate one of the County or City Accountants as the official Council Accountant to perform the function of the City or County Accountant under the Municipal or County Fiscal Control Act insofar as post-budget approval of expenditures is concerned.

ARTICLE II

SECTION 1. Meetings.

Regular meetings of the Council shall be held at such times as shall be determined by the Council. Special meetings of the Council may be called by the Chairman, or by any three members thereof. All meetings shall be open to the public.

At least two days' written notice shall be given of any special meeting of the Council. It shall state the time, place and purpose of the meeting, and may be sent by telegram. Any member may waive notice as to himself.

SECTION 2. Quorum and Vote Required.

Two-thirds (2/3) of the members of the Council shall constitute a quorum at any regular or special meeting of the Council. The affirmative vote of two-thirds of the members of the Council shall be necessary to act favorably on any matter.

SECTION 3. Annual Report.

The Council shall prepare and submit an annual written report of its activities, including a financial statement, to the participating governmental units.

ARTICLE III

SECTION 1. Officers.

At the first regular meeting of the Council, and annually thereafter, the Council shall elect a chairman and vice chairman to serve for one year or until their successors have been duly elected. The Council may also elect such additional officers as the Council finds to be necessary in the proper performance of its duties.

SECTION 2. Duties of Officers.

(a) The chairman shall preside at all meetings of the Council and shall conduct said meetings in an orderly and impartial manner so as to permit a free and full discussion by the membership of such matters as may be brought before the Council. The chairman shall have the same voting rights as other members.

(b) The chairman may appoint such committees as he finds to be necessary or desirable.

(c) The vice chairman shall perform all the duties of the chairman in the absence of the chairman, or in the event of the inability of the chairman to act, and shall perform such other duties as the Council may delegate to him.

(d) All other officers elected by the Council shall perform such duties as may be prescribed by the Council.

ARTICLE IV

SECTION 1. Powers, Duties and Responsibilities of the Council.

The Council, within the limitations of funds and personnel provided by the participating governmental units, shall have the following powers, duties, and responsibilities:

(1) To study such of the following governmental problems common to the governmental units within the Piedmont Triad area as the Council deems appropriate: matters affecting health, safety, welfare, education, economic conditions, and regional development;

(2) To promote cooperative arrangements and coordinated action among the participating governmental units;

(3) To make recommendations for review and action to the participating governmental units and other public agencies which perform functions within the Piedmont Triad area with respect to matters affecting the said area;

(4) To serve as an informational clearing house and as a reviewing agency, with respect to federal, state, and local services or resources available to assist in the solution of the problems;

(5) To request and receive contributions of research assistance from its own agencies, private research organizations, civic foundations, institutions of higher learning and other organizations; to receive and use or expend, in accordance with the provisions of these bylaws, any aid or assistance, monetary or otherwise, which is contributed to the Council from any public or private source, provided that such expenditures must be in accordance with approved budgets;

(6) To employ personnel, purchase equipment, rent office space and enter into contracts to the extent that such activities are authorized by budgets or by specific resolutions duly adopted by all participating governmental units and are within the limits of funds appropriated to the Council by the participating governmental units for such purposes;

(7) To perform and carry out such other powers, duties and responsibilities as may be authorized by Chapter 797 of the 1967 Session Laws (G.S. 160-77.1 through 160-77.6)[3] except insofar as the same may conflict with the provisions of these bylaws; provided, however, the Council shall have no power to levy any tax or to acquire any property by condemnation;

(8) To adopt such rules and regulations relating to the procedures to be followed by the Council as the said Council shall find to be appropriate; and

(9) To act as the official reviewing agency of the participating governmental units for all programs, federal, state or private, requiring regional review.

ARTICLE V

Effective Date.

   These bylaws shall be in full force and effect from and after the date of their adoption by all five of the original participating governmental units as specified herein.

---

[3]Now Part 2, Article 20, of G.S. Chapter 160A.

Rules of Procedure for a Planning Board

PLANNING BOARD RULES OF PROCEDURE

I. GENERAL RULES

The _____ Planning Board shall be governed by the North Carolina General Statutes, the Charter of the *[(City) (County)]* of _____, and other general and special state laws relating to planning in _____, as well as by the ordinance by which this Board was created.

II. OFFICERS AND DUTIES

A. *Chair.* A chair shall be elected by the voting members of the Planning Board. His or her term shall be for one year, and he or she shall be eligible for reelection. The chair shall decide all points of order and procedure, subject to these rules, unless directed otherwise by a majority of the Board in session at the time. The chair shall appoint any committees found necessary to investigate or study matters before the Board.

B. *Vice-Chair.* A vice-chair shall be elected by the Board from among its members in the same manner and for the same term as the chair. He or she shall serve as acting chair in the absence of the chair, and at such times he or she shall have the same powers and duties as the chair.

C. *Secretary.* A secretary shall be appointed by the chair of the Board, either from within or from outside its membership, to hold office during the term of the chair and/or until a successor secretary shall have been appointed. The secretary shall be eligible for reappointment. The secretary, subject to the direction of the chair and the Board, shall keep all records, shall conduct all correspondence of the Board, and shall generally supervise the clerical work of the Board. The secretary shall keep the minutes of every meeting of the Board, which minutes shall be a public record. The minutes shall show the record of all important facts pertaining to each meeting and hearing, every resolution acted upon by the Board, and all votes of Board members upon any resolution or upon the final determination of any question, indicating the names of members absent or failing to vote. If the secretary is chosen from outside the membership of the Board, he or she shall not be eligible to vote upon any matter.

III. MEETINGS.

A. *Regular Meetings.* Regular meetings of the Board shall be held on _____ of each month at _____ A.M./P.M. at _____ provided that if the chair so directs, meetings may be held at any other place in the *[(city) (county)]*.

B. *Special Meetings.* Special meetings of the Board may be called at any time by the chair. At least twenty-four hours' notice of the time and place of special meetings shall be given, by the secretary or the chair, to each member of the Board; provided that this requirement may be waived by action of a majority of all the members.

C. *Cancellation of Meetings.* Whenever there is no business for the Board, the chair may dispense with a regular meeting by giving notice to all the members not less than twenty-four hours before the time set for the meeting.

D. *Quorum.* A quorum shall consist of _____ members of the Board.

E. *Conduct of Meetings.* All meetings shall be open to the public. The order of business at regular meetings shall be as follows: (a) roll call; (b) reading of minutes of previous meeting; (c) reports of committees; (d) unfinished business; (e) new business. Parliamentary procedure shall be in compliance with *Robert's Rules of Order.*

F. *Vote.* The vote of a majority of those members present shall be sufficient to decide matters before the Board, provided a quorum is present. No Board member shall participate in the decision of any matter in which he or she has a personal financial interest.

IV. AMENDMENTS

These rules may, within the limits allowed by law, be amended at any time by an affirmative vote of not less than _____ members of the Board, provided that such amendment shall have first been presented to the membership in writing at a regular or special meeting preceding the meeting at which the vote is taken.

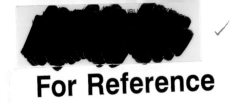